G000128114

the
Creators

INDIVIDUALS OF IRISH FOOD

First published in 2007 by Atrium

Atrium is an imprint of Cork University Press

Youngline Industrial Estate

Pouladuff Road

Togher

Cork

© Dianne Curtin, 2007

All rights reserved. No part of this book may be reprinted or reproduced or utilized
in any electronic, mechanical or other means, now known or hereafter invented,
including photocopying and recording or otherwise, without either the prior written
permission of the Publishers or a licence permitting restricted copying in Ireland
issued by the Irish Copyright Licensing Agency Ltd, The Irish Writers' Centre, 25
Denzille Lane, Dublin 2.

British Library Cataloguing in Publication Data

A CIP catalogue record for this book is available from the British Library.

ISBN: 978-0-9552261-0-6

The author has asserted her moral rights in this work.

Designed at Bite!, Cork City

Printed by Graficas Cems, Navarra, Spain

Photography: © Philip Curtin

the Creators

INDIVIDUALS OF IRISH FOOD

Dianne Curtin

Photography by Philip Curtin

ATRIUM

Dedication

This book is dedicated to my mother Irene. She taught me to be choosy about ingredients, taking me with her every Saturday morning to the market for our weekly shop. She bargained and bantered with fishmongers and butchers in order to get the very best quality. Afterwards, she'd take me for tea and sandwiches in the market café. So many of my early food recollections revolve around her being in the kitchen at home, her flour-covered hands, and the way she lovingly pickled roll-mops for my father every Friday, despite the smell of vinegar and fish pervading all corners of the house. And, of course, her apple tarts, fruit cakes, meat and potato pies, Yorkshire Puddings, and the best beef stew and dumplings ever, all now only ever enjoyed in my memories.

Thanks Mum.

Also, for Phil's father John Curtin, who sadly passed away in April 2007. We know you were really looking forward to seeing this book in print, and that you would be tremendously proud.

Contents

Introduction

The gourmet revolution in Ireland first kicked off over thirty years ago. It came as a result of those adventurous few, brave enough to take the first tentative, unsteady, steps into farmhouse-based productions. In Cork, the original food pioneers were long-time farmers looking to diversify and make the most of what they already grew or farmed. Others were 'blow-ins', often with connections to the county, who had returned, settled and started to think sideways about how to make a living here. From these small beginnings, the area now has the largest concentration of food producers in the country. Cork's national and international reputation as a food region is enviable.

This book celebrates a selection of those who made this so. Some were there at the very beginning. Others have joined the ranks in recent years. But all share some simple characteristics. Each has total commitment, dedication, and passion for their food, and how it comes about. Every one of them has real reason to get up in the morning and go about their daily business of bringing the best to the tables of those who seek it out.

While it's all too easy to stack a shopping trolley high with cheap groceries, some of whose origins are questionable – if not highly debatable – and have little interest in whether what we have bought is good, bad or indifferent, there comes a time when the average shopper will stop and think. I hope these stories will make that happen more often. Cork is blessed with great things to eat, made right here on its doorstep. Home-cured charcuterie and smoked fish, fresh meat and poultry – it's all here. Compare, if you will, the flavour and texture of a wedge of local handmade farmhouse cheese that has taken many months to mature to that of a mass-produced, machine-made imported block. My guess is, that for even the most average consumer with no particular food persuasions, there will be no comparison. Alright, the farmhouse cheese will cost more. After all, it has taken so much extra time, care and manpower to produce. It has its own individual personality. They say money can't buy everything. But in food terms it will certainly buy the pleasure derived from eating something that has been an investment of devotion for the people who made it.

Many producers in this book work on a very small scale. Cheese Masters Bill Hogan and Sean Ferry, for example, choose to make just a few of their unique Swiss-style cheeses weekly and only in summer, when sweet unpasteurized milk is available. Caroline and Eddie Robinson grow their chemical-free vegetables on a small-holding, preferring to supply a range of seasonal varieties in limited quantities over cultivating the acres of crops that large supermarkets demand. Some producers have succeeded in expanding into bigger businesses, without compromising on quality. Poultry farmers Eugene and Helena Hickey, whose barn-reared duck production started with a flock of just 30, now provide birds to selected franchise supermarkets, butchers and restaurants on a year-round basis. Sally Barnes, Anthony Creswell and Frank Hederman are three of Ireland's most prominent artisan producers of smoked salmon – all with very differing views on how best to reach the perfect end-product. Put the three of them in a room together and the ensuing discussion is likely to be very lively indeed! That's what makes them unique, and why their creations offer individuality and diversity. You may wonder if there can be any real difference. After all, it's the same fish isn't it? One fish, yes. But three very different approaches, to lend marvellous subtleties of style, taste and texture, only discovered in the joy of eating.

Cornie Bohane and Colin Whooley are harvesters of finest quality fish and shellfish from local coastal waters. In doing their jobs each day, they must contend with all that nature's awesome power throws at them. Cornie comes from a family whose heritage is embedded in fishing for its living. He is one of a dying breed. The fishing industry in this country is being killed off quietly by ever more stringent laws that can see a fisherman have his gear, and even his freedom, removed in an instant. Once the likes of Cornie disappear, it will be difficult to find men of his calibre to take over the role. These days, who wants to battle the severity of a sometimes unforgiving ocean? That's the easy part, in a fisherman's eyes. But the severity of an official body that does not seem to want to keep a long-standing and essential food industry alive? Now that is a different kettle of *poisson*. Not many men exist in the business already, and there will be even less coming forward in years to come.

Every person featured on these pages has different circumstances. But what really binds them together is their drive to get it right, above all else. Like acclaimed painters or sculptors, food creators aim for the highest possible standards, do not accept compromise or low-level thinking, always strive to do better, and are never satisfied unless they have realized their own personal goals. Making top-quality bread, patisserie, or chocolates, rearing livestock in a traditional, humane and caring way, growing superlative, seasonal fruit and vegetables without chemical help, and putting out to sea every day, regardless of red tape and black clouds, are talents that can't really be taught. Okay, you might argue, for instance, that the rudiments of farming, horticulture, baking and the like are ones that anybody could go to college to learn. But not everyone who holds a paintbrush becomes Picasso. It takes a creative perfectionist to fine-tune those basic taught skills and turn them into an art form. Intuition, obsession, enthusiasm, infatuation, excitement, intensity and a deep, deep love for what is being achieved must come into play. For the people in this book, their work is not just a job. It is a way of life. And it never stops being worthwhile.

From Land and Field

From Land and Field

Drive Ireland's winding country roads on a hot summer's day, just after silage has been cut, and pastures of pale greeny-gold provide the view. Repeat the same journey in autumn, with rain washed fields of earthy moss or dark racing green for company. In the crispness of winter, frost-nipped emerald and mist shrouded sea-green acres stretch for miles around. This land, ever growing, ever changing with the seasons, is the country's beating heart.

Ireland's grazing is second to none. The Cork region is prolific. Well managed beef herds like Angus, Herefords and Piedmontese, roaming free in natural, sweet and protein rich grassland, munch their way to becoming tasty table material. In the hands of the right farmer, slaughterer and butcher, and left to hang to develop mature flavour and tender succulence, the meat these animals yield is a joy to cook with, a gourmet experience to eat. The county's fertile and diverse terrain is also of huge benefit to other livestock reared with good feasting in mind. Pigs, lambs, geese and chickens all gain flavour from the wild herbs, sweet clover, meadow flowers and hedgerow fruits that form part of the daily diet of an animal produced free range in this kind of environment.

Under the cover of Cork's familiar green blanket lies another treasure in her soft, moist, rich soil. Knowledgeable and committed fresh-produce growers, wise to what nature has already provided, turn that raw material to their own advantage. The successful recipe for great tasting, wholesome fruit and vegetables includes natural bounty, seasoned with the grower's expertise, and his inherent intuition for knowing just how this land works best.

The Creators in this section use land and field to the best of their advantage. And their end results bear witness to just how fruitful the forces of nature, combined with the exact amount of human intervention, can be.

Caroline and Eddie Robinson – Vegetable Growers

In Templemartin, just outside Bandon, set up on a hill, a cosy farmhouse and 30 acres is home to Caroline and Eddie Robinson. They work the land in the old-fashioned way to grow a huge variety of seasonal vegetables without the use of chemicals.

Situated on its majestic river, Bandon is rooted in over four hundred years of history. Throughout those years, it has embraced change on many fronts, leaving behind its origins as a walled town of Protestant domination to become the progressive, bustling business centre of today. In contrast to its past segregation, Bandon now has a diverse community, a mix of born and bred Bandonians whose heritage goes back centuries, and those who have adopted the town and surrounding area as home. Caroline and Eddie Robinson chose to make a small holding in the fertile countryside their permanent address in the mid-nineties.

Caroline, born in Kenya, came to Ireland aged three, when her Irish parents returned to Carrigaline. She remembers enjoying home-grown vegetables from the small garden of their house on the outskirts of Cork City. 'My father was a keen organic grower in his spare time', she says. He was also an avid collector of the Soil Association's magazines. As a youngster, she read them and still has his whole collection, dating back to 1962. 'Times have changed now', says Caroline, pointing out that back then the concept of organic farming was perhaps a mite idealistic.

Meeting Eddie was the result of a trip back to Kenya in 1987. Caroline's husband, a charming, good-humoured man with a solid knowledge of his business, is as dedicated as she is to growing the best produce in a natural way. It's almost impossible to believe that the guy who now happily gathers trailer loads of manure for fertilizing and begs garden clippings from friends for his mulch pile was once, as Caroline puts it, 'a conventional farmer'. 'The first glimpse my family had of Eddie was a photo of him sitting on his huge chemical sprayer. They must have got an awful shock', she laughs. For some years in Kenya, the couple farmed barley and wheat together, fighting soaring land rents and living without subsidies. But the EU grain donation to Africa made it impossible for them to survive and they eventually returned to Ireland in 1995.

Brought up on traditional growing methods and already convinced they were the way to go, Caroline set about with her husband to get their land ready. 'Soil quality is everything', she says, 'Eddie fertilizes with organic manure and uses crop rotation, which is important so land can regenerate itself.'

It's easy to be flabbergasted at the amount of weeds on the Robinsons' farm, and it sets the mind wondering just how those vegetables struggle through. But for anyone who has ever tried growing anything without chemicals, even on the smallest of scales, it eases the guilt when reality dawns that no sprays mean lots of weeds. Suddenly, it doesn't seem a battle anymore. As Caroline says, 'Weeds are difficult to control, but they tell a story about the soil and they don't stop vegetables growing. I always think that if you have to get down on your hands and knees to get rid of them, the weeds have won!'

Whatever way it works naturally, these plentiful but unwanted soil squatters certainly don't affect productivity. The farm yields a mix of outdoor and tunnel-grown crops. Outside, bushy carrot plants and broccoli stems rub shoulders with crisp, squeaky leaved cabbages, and a regiment of leeks and onions. The tunnels nurture rows of colourful salad leaves and, in the height of summer, tomato plants hanging with trusses of ripe, heavy fruit, unable to keep themselves standing upright without supporting twine to bear the weight.

Where potatoes are concerned, Caroline and Eddie choose varieties that take well to chemical-free methods and grow later in the season to escape the worst of summer blight that wipes out plants that aren't sprayed. Years of experience, combined with the couple's shared love of real horticultural practice, ensures a healthy and prolific harvest of big potatoes with smoothest blemish-free skins that just break when they are gently steamed, revealing a flirtatious glimpse of floury innards. A piping hot bowlful simply shouts out for a good spoonful of creamy Irish butter to melt seductively on top.

All the Robinsons' vegetables have an intensity of flavour non-existent in those mass produced. A visit to the couple on a warm summer afternoon, talking food, farming and the meaning of life in general, is a pleasure heightened only by the bag of heavily scented, intensely flavoured tomatoes, or voluptuously full, ready-to-be-popped fresh peas given generously as a going-home gift. Their salad leaves put anything in a shop-bought puffer bag in the shade. Mizuna, rocket, oakleaf and the many other varieties Caroline crams into her loosely termed 'salad mix' have the kind of taste you can never expect from their supermarket counterparts.

As a pro-active member of the Green Party and a major player at the Cork Free Choice Consumer Group, founded by the original campaigner for good wholesome food, Myrtle Allen of Ballymaloe House, Caroline is instrumental in trying to effect change for small holders and market traders all over the county. With Myrtle at its helm, the group was set up to form a network with other like-minded growers, and as a source of information for the general public. Guest speakers address the regular monthly meetings and keep consumers informed of just what is on offer food-wise in Cork. Caroline sells the couple's produce directly to customers from her stall at Cornmarket Street's farmer's market in the city and the weekly market in Macroom, firmly believing that this way of selling has re-forged that long-lost connection between buyer and grower. 'We couldn't supply supermarkets that want only one or two things on a consistent basis', she says. 'Everything is seasonal, so customers know they won't always find what they came for, but buy what's here instead.'

For a cook, the great thing about shopping this way is the surprise element. You never know what you will find. The trip to purchase a head of green cabbage may well conclude instead with a basketful of tender baby leeks or a bunch of newly dug young carrots, moist earth still clinging to their slender forms. It's all about going with it – and making life in the kitchen just that little bit unpredictable. And thanking heaven for producers like Caroline and Eddie who provide the raw materials of inspiration.

Caroline and Eddie's Vegetables

IN SPRING AND SUMMER:
Huge selection of salad leaves, including rocket, oakleaf, mizuna, lollo rosso, cos, beetroot, tomatoes, spring onions, baby carrots, peas and beans.

IN AUTUMN AND WINTER:
Unusual varieties of potatoes, broccoli, leeks, main crop carrots, parsnips, cauliflowers, onions, and cabbages.

Vegetable Couscous

Couscous is a dish popular in Morocco and Algiers, its name taken from the tiny pieces of grain that form the basis of the dish. Couscous is often made in a special pot called a couscoussier, which consists of a bottom pan to hold a chunky, flavourful vegetable broth, and a top steamer rather similar to a big colander, where traditionally the grains are set to plump up over the vegetables simmering gently beneath. The couscous is served on a platter often decorated with a few sultanas or pine nuts, with the broth doled out into individual bowls and some spicy harissa – a hot red chilli paste – on the side. This is optional though. For meat eaters, a few skewers of grilled lamb or chicken chunks are also welcome additions. This recipe soaks the couscous first for speed, then it can be heated through over the broth or in a microwave.

Soak couscous in just enough water to cover until all is absorbed and grains are tender. Meanwhile, heat oil in a pan and fry onion, garlic, carrot, parsnip and courgette until slightly softened. Pour over chopped tomatoes and stock. Add whole chilli. Bring to bubbling and simmer until vegetables are tender. Stir in chickpeas and simmer for a few minutes to heat through. Season. Place soaked couscous in a steamer over the simmering broth and steam through for the last few minutes until piping hot, or microwave on high in one-minute blasts. Scatter pinenuts and sultanas into couscous, drizzle with a little olive oil and season. Serve couscous and vegetable broth separately, with a little bowl of harissa on the table so diners can help themselves.

SERVES 4

- 225g/8oz couscous
- 2 tbsp olive oil
- 1 onion, peeled and chopped
- 2 cloves garlic, peeled and crushed
- 1 carrot, and 1 small parsnip, peeled and chopped
- 1 courgette, in chunks
- 400g can chopped tomatoes
- 300ml/½pt vegetable stock
- 1 whole red chilli
- 400g can chickpeas, drained salt and freshly ground black pepper
- 2 tbsp toasted pinenuts
- 1 tbsp plump sultanas
- Harissa paste for serving

Broccoli and Gorgonzola Tart

When is a quiche not a quiche? When it's a tart, I say. An authentic quiche as we know it, which came from France way back when it was hip to eat it, should contain only eggs, cream and maybe some chopped bacon. Trouble is, like all good things, quiche was over-marketed and the term is now synonymous with any savoury egg flan, no matter what the filling. So this recipe is definitely a tart – albeit a creamy, eggy one, but packed with tiny florets of broccoli and some piquant Gorgonzola encased in crisp buttery pastry.

For the pastry, place all the ingredients in a processor and whiz to form a ball. Wrap and chill for 20 minutes in the fridge. Roll out on a floured board to fit a 20cm/8in. loose-bottomed quiche tin. Fill case with greaseproof and baking beans and bake blind in a pre-heated oven, Gas 6/400°F/200°C for 10 minutes or until just set but not yet browned. Remove from oven, lift out greaseproof and baking beans and cool slightly.

Blanch broccoli florets for a minute in lightly salted boiling water. Drain and pat dry with kitchen towel. Break up the cheese and sprinkle in the base of the pastry case. Strew broccoli over this. Beat eggs with milk and cream. Season with freshly ground black pepper – you probably won't need salt as the cheese is salty. Pour mix over cheese and broccoli. Return to oven, Gas 6/400°F/200°C for a further 30 minutes or until pastry is golden and crisp and tart is set and browned.

SERVES 4

FOR THE PASTRY:
· 175g/6oz plain flour, sifted
· 100g/4oz butter, chilled and in cubes
· 1 egg
· pinch salt

FOR THE TART:
· 100g/4oz broccoli, cut in tiny florets
· 175g/6oz Gorgonzola
· 3 free range eggs
· 150ml/¼pt milk
· 150ml/¼pt cream
· freshly ground black pepper

Carrot and Cork Gin Soup

Probably the best time to make this smooth but subtly spicy soup is in early winter when main crop carrots are plentiful and the shorter days call for a steaming bowlful of something revitalizing to keep you going. Cork Dry Gin is a must here – a splash enhances the sweetness of the carrot and gives the inner person a little boost too. Teeny golden croutons garnish the finished soup.

Heat oil in a pan and add onion and garlic. Cook gently to soften. Add chilli flakes, carrots and potatoes and toss around for a minute more. Pour over stock. Add bouquet garni and bring to bubbling. Simmer for a good 20 minutes, covered, or until carrots are soft enough to puree. Remove bouquet garni. Puree smooth with a hand blender or in a processor, adding more stock if the consistency should need thinning. Stir in gin. Season with sea salt and freshly ground black pepper and add coriander.

While the soup is simmering, heat sunflower oil in a large frying pan and fry bread cubes until golden and crisp. Remove with a slotted spoon and drain on kitchen paper. Serve soup in a big tureen scattered with golden croutons.

SERVES 4

· 2 tbsp olive oil
· 1 small onion, peeled and chopped
· 1 clove garlic, peeled and crushed
  pinch dried red chilli flakes
· 4 decent-sized carrots, peeled and chopped (about 350g/12oz peeled weight)
· 2 smallish floury potatoes, peeled and in chunks
· 1.1ltr/2pt chicken or vegetable stock (approx.)
· 1 fresh bouquet garni with bay leaf, parsley and thyme sprigs
· 1–2 tbsp Cork Dry Gin (to taste)
· sea salt and freshly ground black pepper
· 1 tbsp finely chopped fresh coriander

FOR THE CROUTONS:
· sunflower oil for shallow frying
· 2 thin slices white bread, crusts removed and cut into small cubes

Summer Tomato Salad

The headiness of long summer days are epitomized in this fabulously simple salad which relies on juicy, ripe tomatoes like Caroline and Eddie's home-grown ones to be anywhere near the mark. No frilly leaves adorn it. Only sliced tomatoes, a few thinly sliced onion rings and some torn fresh basil have a role here – dressed generously with extra virgin olive oil and splashes of dark, sweet balsamic vinegar. A word about tomatoes. Keep them away from the fridge. Buy little and often and leave them in the fruit bowl on a kitchen worktop. Refrigerated tomatoes lose flavour and take on a certain hardness so opposed to what these fruits should have when at their best. For the dressing, I like the deep green Cretan olive oil or you could use a Tuscan oil which has a lovely pepperiness.

Thinly slice tomatoes using a small sharp knife and arrange on a large platter with room to spare round the edges so the salad isn't cramped. Cut the onion into fine rings. Arrange over tomatoes. Tear the basil leaves roughly and scatter over. Season with sea salt and freshly ground black pepper. Drizzle generously with extra virgin olive oil and drip the balsamic vinegar all around, letting some run on to the plate for effect! Serve absolutely straightaway.

SERVES 4 AS A SIDE DISH OR TWO AS A LIGHT LUNCH WITH BREAD

- 8 ripe red tomatoes
- 1 small onion, peeled
- good few basil leaves (at least 8)
- sea salt and freshly ground black pepper
- extra virgin olive oil
- balsamic vinegar

Peas with Bacon in the French Style

This is based on the classic *Petit Pois à la Française* but without the thickened sauce. Fresh summer peas are dressed with fresh cream instead. Serve this vegetable dish with a Sunday roast leg of lamb.

Heat oil in a pan and fry bacon crisp. Add stock and bring to bubbling. Add peas, lettuce and spring onions and cook, covered, until peas are tender. This takes only a few moments when the peas are really fresh and small. Stir in cream and seasoning. Sprinkle with mint.

SERVES 4

· 1 tbsp sunflower oil
· 4 rashers streaky bacon, chopped
· 150ml/¼pt chicken or vegetable stock
· 450g/1lb fresh peas, podded weight
· a crisp heart of lettuce, in wedges
· 8 thin spring onions, trimmed into lengths
· 4 tbsp cream
· sea salt and freshly ground black pepper
· few fresh mint leaves, chopped

Garden Greens Tumble

The French and Spanish favour this way of serving a mix of green vegetables in summer. Simplicity itself, it relies on the freshest ingredients. Choose any combination from fresh broad beans, peas, thin green beans and runner beans – or have them all as I've done here.

Blanch all the vegetables separately in lightly salted boiling water. The beans will need a minute or two longer than the peas or broad beans. Drain and remove outer skins from broad beans. Place all together in a big bowl. For the dressing, mix olive oil and lemon juice in a bowl. Season. Pour over salad and add lemon zest and mint. Toss to coat and serve immediately.

SERVES 4

· 100g/4oz thin green beans, topped and tailed
· 100g/4oz runner beans, topped, tailed and cut into long strips
· 175g/6oz fresh peas, podded weight
· 350g/12oz fresh broad beans, podded weight

FOR THE DRESSING:
· 4 tbsp extra virgin olive oil
· juice of a lemon
· sea salt and freshly ground black pepper
· strips of zest of a lemon
· 2 tbsp fresh mint leaves, torn

More Vegetable Ideas

- Caroline and Eddie harvest their vegetables just before going to market, so they are fresh and packed with nutrients for their customers. Try to retain the nutrients in any fresh vegetables by lightly cooking them in a vitamin-friendly style. Steaming is great for greens like broccoli, asparagus and tender young cabbage. Peas can be cooked in stock, which is then part of the sauce of the dish, as in the 'Peas with bacon' recipe, or blanched quickly in lightly salted boiling water. Young fresh peas can be eaten raw in a salad. In fact, when I'm podding them, almost always it's 'One for me, one for the pot'. Stir frying works well for carrots, leeks and runner beans.

- Roast potatoes are meant to be crackly and crisp on the outside and fluffy within. Achieve this by first blanching the peeled potato chunks in lightly salted water for a few moments. Then drain well in a colander. Shake the colander of drained potatoes to roughen up the edges. While potatoes are blanching, heat 4 tbsp sunflower oil or 3 tbsp beef dripping for 900g/2lb weight of potatoes, in a roasting tray. Carefully place the roughed-up potatoes in the tray of hot fat, spooning some over. Return to preheated oven Gas 6/400°F/200°C for 40 minutes or until tender and crisp. Remember to turn the spuds during cooking. Season with flakes of sea salt, and freshly ground black pepper.

- My aunt, a great cook, used to steam a whole cauliflower then serve it in a big bowl with a creamy home-made cheddar cheese sauce poured over. It always looked spectacular coming to the table. As an alternative to cheese sauce, this gutsy Mediterranean mix of olive oil, garlic and anchovies makes a good swap. Choose a medium-sized cauliflower, and trim away most of the green leaves, leaving just the ones that furl around the curds at the very centre. Trim base, then cut a cross in it so that the heat will penetrate up into the centre. Either cook the cauliflower in a deep pan of salted boiling water, covered, until it is just tender, then drain well, or set it in a steamer over a pan of boiling water, which keeps vitamins better but takes a bit longer. Meanwhile warm 150ml/¼pt extra virgin olive oil in a pan and add 2 cloves peeled, crushed garlic and 4 finely chopped anchovy fillets. Squeeze in the juice of half a lemon and season with lots of freshly ground black pepper. Finally add 1 tbsp chopped parsley. When the caulilflower is ready, place it in a large dish, pour the sauce over and around. Scatter with extra freshly chopped parsley.

John Howard – Fruit Farmer

A gentle breeze blows through the fields and grassland in the countryside around the village of Rathcormac in North Cork. In the midst of this rural setting, acres of soft fruit plants are in full swing, their plump and juicy yields swelling all the time with light summer rain. Strawberries, blackberries, raspberries and gooseberries are just a few of the gems to be found at Sunnyside Fruit Farm, a jewel in County Cork's crown of good fresh produce.

There's something to be said for enjoying a bowl of soft berries in the height of summer, when they are home grown and of the utmost high quality. Eating imported fruit in the depths of winter is never so satisfying. John Howard has been growing fruit on his thirty acres of land in Rathcormac since 1983. And, at this stage, he's something of an expert. It shows in his repertoire, which alongside traditional soft fruits, includes golden raspberries, tayberries, loganberries, black, white and redcurrants, and blueberries – all of the most exquisite quality.

This man's experience was first gleaned working for a fruit grower in Glanmire, where he spent a number of years learning the business inside out. In the early eighties, thinking it was about time to 'take the plunge' as he puts it, John started his own set up. His intention was always to keep down the use of chemicals in fruit growing, though as he says, 'It's an almost impossible task to grow fruit of any quality and quantity without them. The risk of disease and pests makes life very difficult.' As a keen conservationist though, John was anxious to keep sprays and pesticides to an absolute minimum, preferring instead more natural methods of deterring the bugs – simply by letting Mother Nature do her own thing.

With an eye to this, John became a member of the Rural Environmental Protection scheme (Reps) for farmers who use low chemical intervention. The scheme dictates strict guidelines in retaining the natural features of the

countryside, and encouraging wildlife. But these come as no hardship to this man, since he's a wildlife lover and keen birdwatcher. He has specially built two large ponds on his land, where frogs, newts, Lamprey eels and all manner of water life reside. Outside the kitchen window, the neatly kept garden is home to blue tits, numerous finches and sparrows, feeding from peanut holders, generous scraps on the bird table – and, of course, the insects and grubs that would otherwise be nibbling the berries. Beyond the garden wall, the surrounding fields are the regular hunting grounds of hen harriers, merlin hawks, sparrow hawks and two types of owl. As a part of the Reps commitment, John also plants crops specially to sustain and feed wildlife and leaves these unharvested. All of this helps to keep a balance in nature and minimize the application of chemicals in farming.

Work on the farm begins early in the year. Even on the wettest days, the ground is being prepared and made ready for early spring plantings. Existing plants are pruned to bring on strong and healthy growth later in the year. John says 'In fruit growing, there is a lot of work. Once you accept that and are prepared for it, that's half the job. The most successful weeding is done by hand. There is no other way, and weeds are our biggest problem.' With proper preparation, time and dedication, however, the farm will be productive enough at the peak of season to require the help of an extra fifty pairs of hands to pick the crop through the summer months. 'The berries must be handpicked to ensure none are damaged. It's important we use pickers who handle the fruit perfectly', says John.

It's hard for anyone who has never really attempted to garden to imagine what effort and labour is ultimately involved in producing fruit of the quality of Sunnyside's. But the wide range of berries speaks for itself. Strawberry plants are heavy with succulent scarlet fruit. Redcurrant, blackcurrant and whitecurrant bushes dangle with stems of berries that look like precious gemstones, glinting in the sunshine. John's selection of gooseberry bushes hang with fat, translucent green berries, which beg to be baked in a pie, poached for a crumble or stewed with sugar to enjoy with fresh cream.

In 2005, John opened a new farm shop to replace the original, housed in a small section of the outbuilding used for packing and preparation. The new premises on site has given him more space to display fresh fruit and other fruit-based items, away from any other working areas. In June, July and August, the shop stocks freshly picked berries, jams, chutneys and health drinks, all local specialities. During the summer, John makes the trip each Saturday morning to Midleton market, to sell his berries direct to the public from a market stall. Out of season, a good selection of Sunnyside's berries are available frozen, prepared on the farm using modern new equipment. Whole berries come in mixed bags or as single varieties, and defrost beautifully for hot pies, crumbles, cobblers and other warming desserts.

John Howard is a gently spoken, dedicated farmer, whose love of the countryside, wildlife and environment has driven him to producing the best possible fruit without encroaching on nature, or ruining the landscape. His Sunnyside berries are succulent, juicy and hand harvested just at the peak of ripeness. It doesn't matter how you eat them – whether they are arranged elegantly on a cheesecake, tumbled rampantly over a Pavlova, standing upright to attention on a glamorous tart, or simply heaped in a bowl and drizzled with best Irish cream. One thing is certain. Every fragrant, fruity mouthful is the very essence of summer.

Sunnyside's Fruit Harvest

IN SPRING
Gooseberries, strawberries, raspberries, golden raspberries, tayberries, blueberries, loganberries, blackberries, red, white and blackcurrants, all available fresh.

IN WINTER:
All the above (depending on stocks) are available in single variety frozen packs or mixed bags.

Sparkling Strawberries in Melon Cups

Fresh strawberries marinated with icing sugar and and mint served in melon cups, topped up with sweet sparkling wine. These are a bit seventies, but nevertheless delicious! Use small melons, such as fragrant Charantais or Ogen. Make sure they are ripe and juicy. A good sniff should tell you.

Hull, rinse and pat berries dry, then slice. Place them in a bowl. Sprinkle over icing sugar and mint and toss to mix. Halve melons and scoop out seeds. Fill each melon cup with berries, then divide the wine between the four cups. Serve immediately, decorated with mint sprigs.

SERVES 4

· 450g/1lb ripe strawberries
· 2 tbsp icing sugar, sifted
· small handful of fresh mint leaves, chopped
· 2 ripe Charentais or Ogen melons
· about a glass of sweet sparkling wine (Asti Spumante is good)
· mint sprigs for decoration

Summer Hedgerow Pudding

A timeless dessert, this has made the menus of some very sprauncy eating establishments in its time, and can still wow a bunch of home dinner guests with its glamour. Serve it with rich Irish pouring cream or be extravagant and go for a top-quality, bought vanilla ice cream if you want. Scoop it out of the tub using two dessertspoons briefly dipped in hot water, and shape the scoops between the two spoons to make pointy ovals, or 'quenelles' for a bit of a show-off presentation. Decorate plates with flourishes of mint.

SERVES 4

· 900g/2lb mixed fresh summer berries (if using large strawberries, hull and halve them first)
· 2 tbsp sugar (or to taste)
· 150ml/¼pt water
· approximately 10 large slices white bread, crusts removed
· mint sprigs for decoration

Place fruit in a pan with sugar and water and simmer gently until softened but still with shape. Strain and reserve juice. Cut a circle of bread to fit the base of a pudding bowl big enough to hold all the berries and pop this in place. Cut another circle for the top of the basin, then trim remaining slices into fat strips. Line sides of basin with these, overlapping slightly. Spoon a little juice into the base then pack in fruit, pressing down well. Drizzle with a little more juice and place bread lid on top. Bring remaining juice to the boil and simmer until reduced and syrupy. Cool and pour over pud, then cover with film, cover with a saucer and pop a weight on top (a full food can will do). Chill overnight then carefully unmould onto a plate and decorate with mint.

Raspberry Ripples

This is one of those ideas for when there really is no time for making a more sophisticated pudding. It does need a little chilling, but if time is really of the essence, make sure the cream and yogurt are well chilled and you should just about get away with serving it straight away.

Puree raspberries with orange juice and sugar to taste. Whip cream to soft peaks and stir in yogurt. Carefully fold in raspberry puree in ripples. Spoon into glasses and pile extra fresh raspberries on top. Chill until required.

SERVES 4

· 225g/8oz raspberries
· juice of an orange
· icing sugar
· 300ml/½pt cream
· 150ml/¼pt thick Greek yogurt
· extra whole raspberries for topping

Strawberry Salad with Balsamic Vinegar and Fresh Parmesan

In Italy, they eat strawberries with really good, matured balsamic vinegar and that's where I first tried it. The vinegar needs to be aged so it has that luscious, sweet sour taste. I've added the parmesan which I think works as a sort of cheese course after a meal where you haven't got a pud. In fact, it combines the two very nicely. You could also use Gabriel or Desmond cheese for this.

SERVES 4

· 450g/1lb fresh, ripe strawberries, hulled, rinsed and patted dry
· good, aged balsamic vinegar
· freshly ground black pepper
· a knobbly wedge of fresh parmesan cheese

Halve the strawberries if large. Place in a bowl. Shake over a few drips of the balsamic vinegar – not too heavy handedly, and season with freshly ground black pepper. Toss lightly with finger tips, then pop onto serving plates. Serve shavings or slivers of fresh cheese, which have been hacked off a large knobbly chunk, on the side. Or alternatively, place the cheese on the cheese board with a parmesan knife and let people hack off their own.

Duck Breasts with Fresh Redcurrant Vinaigrette

This might seem like an odd combination, but the richness of the duck meat actually appreciates a little alert acidity from ripe redcurrants. The dressing is just warm, so the berries infuse their flavour before pouring over the pink cooked duck breast fillets. I think these make an elegant starter, with perhaps a fishy main course to follow.

Heat a dry heavy bottomed frying pan over high heat until searingly hot. Season duck breasts, place in pan skin side down, and cook until browned and their fat begins to run. Turn over to brown other sides, then lower heat, cover and cook until meat is well browned but still pink and juicy in the centre. Prod them with a fingertip. They should feel firm but with a little 'give' in the centre. Alternatively you can test one by piercing with a skewer or the point of a sharp knife, but don't cut it too much or all the juice will escape.

While the duck breasts are cooking, mix oils with mustard and vinegar in a pan. Add redcurrants and warm gently until they just pop. Season and add a little more sunflower oil if the flavour is too sharp. Stir in thyme.

Remove duck breasts from pan and place on a chopping board. Leave for a moment or two until cool enough to handle, then slice each breast thickly into four or five slices, diagonally. Arrange on warmed plates with lamb's tongue lettuce on the side. Spoon a little dressing over each and serve immediately, decorated with small sprigs of fresh redcurrants.

SERVES 4

· 4 duck breast fillets
· sea salt and freshly ground black pepper

FOR THE DRESSING:
· 6 tbsp sunflower oil
· 2 tbsp walnut oil
· 2 tsp Dijon mustard
· 2 tbsp red wine vinegar
· 2 tbsp ripe redcurrants
· sea salt and freshly ground black pepper
· 1 tsp fresh thyme leaves
· lamb's tongue lettuce and fresh redcurrant sprigs to serve

Other Ideas for Fresh Summer Berries

- Use fresh strawberries and whipped cream to fill an ordinary sponge cake for a special tea, or as a birthday cake. For the sponge, cream 175g/6oz softened butter with 175g/6oz caster sugar until light and fluffy. Sift 175g/6oz self-raising flour into a bowl. Beat three medium free range eggs. Add these a little at a time, alternately with a spoonful of flour mix, beating well between each addition. Continue until eggs are all incorporated then fold in the remaining flour. Add a splash of milk to form a soft dropping consistency. Pour the mix equally into two lined and buttered sandwich tins. Bake in a preheated oven, Gas 5/375°F/190°C for 20 minutes or until golden, well risen and firm to the touch. Remove from oven and cool slightly. Turn out on to wire racks, peel off baking parchment and cool completely. Place one cake, smooth side up, on a cake stand or plate, and spread with a couple of tablespoons of strawberry preserve, then 4 tbsp whipped cream, and 100g/4oz fresh sliced strawberries. Pop remaining sponge on top. Sift over icing sugar, pop a large blob of cream in the centre, and tumble a few whole strawberries on for decoration.

- A mix of colourful summer berries make a great table centre piece, served in a stunning glass bowl. The only go-with necessary is whipped cream, perhaps flavoured with a sweet fruit liqueur, such as Grand Marnier or Cointreau. For 300ml/½pt whipped cream, sift in 1 tbsp icing sugar and a good splash of either liqueur. Stir together and serve immediately with the berries.

- Early summer mornings are made even better when you add a few fresh whole berries to the usual bowl of cereal. I love them, especially with an organic luxury muesli mix, available from most good health food shops, which I think is not as sweet as its mass-produced cousin. Thick Greek yogurt is very good with this too.

Eugene and Helena Hickey – Duck and Goose Producers

There are few places that possess the wild wind-swept beauty of the West Cork coast. A visit on a winter day, well wrapped to beat the chill, for a walk in the rugged countryside around Roaring Water Bay, is as enchanting as any taken in the height of summer. From the right spot, you can glance up to the dew-soaked green fields behind, and see them speckled with white cotton wool balls. Look more closely, and the cotton wool balls move. They are the snowy-feathered free range Christmas geese of Eugene and Helena Hickey.

The Hickey's 110-acre holding at Skeaghanore, Ballydehob, overlooking this spectacular bay and its coastal rocky outcrop, was Eugene's childhood home. His wife Helena says, 'Gene's family always kept a few geese here for Christmas.' The couple carried on the tradition, along with looking after their dairy and beef herds. In 1994, after professional advice from Teagasc, the West Cork Leader Co-op, which supports local enterprise, offered help and the Hickeys set up the poultry business in earnest, initially starting with ducks – just 30 in their first flock.

With a decent product to sell and a will to succeed, Eugene took the step of visiting the region's shops and restaurants, encouraging their proprietors to take one or two ducks to try. Chefs and butchers liked what they got. 'We had a great response, especially from local shops who supported us right from the start', says Helena. From small beginnings, Skeaghanore Duck now produces birds on a year-round basis, and the company is part of the prestigious West Cork Fuchsia brand of local foods, well known far beyond the boundaries of the area, and whose name is taken from the wild pink-blossomed fuchsia bushes that grow profusely along every lane and boreen.

Skeaghanore ducklings are reared in warm deep straw-bedded barns, cereal fed, and matured to develop flavour. All the processing is dealt with on site, so the finished birds go from farm to fork without stress. These ducks are meaty and tasty, producing a satisfying roast with delectable, crisp skin. As well as whole birds, the Hickeys also supply magrets, which have become de rigueur on the menus of many restaurants. The plump duck breast fillets are convenient for pan frying or quick roasting, with no bones to deal with at the table. Duck legs are also available, and perfect for a home-made Confit of Duck, where they are salted, cooked slowly in extra duck fat, then sealed in kilner jars to preserve them in the classic French style. This dish, like many others before it, was invented by the thrifty French housewives of old, who knew only too well the value of preserving whatever fresh produce was around, to be savoured in times of scarcity.

Alongside the ever-growing and hugely successful duck production, the Hickeys decided to redevelop the goose farming side of the business, coinciding with a growing demand for these birds in recent Christmasses. The couple now raise over 300 geese annually for the Christmas market. Centuries before the domestication of turkeys, geese were the choice for a festive feast. They have always had celebratory links. Michaelmas Day, 29 September, heralded the start of the season and, traditionally, a goose was roasted, usually after having dined out on rich pickings in a newly harvested cornfield beforehand. The ancient custom of serving goose on this date still goes on throughout the world. For many, Christmas is all the better for the grandeur of a majestic, golden goose. As the bird cooks, the fat melts to baste the rich dark meat and crisp the skin. Old wives saved 'goose grease' to rub on chests for winter chills. Modern goose cooks are never so generous, appreciating the fat's culinary preciousness, pouring it from the tray during cooking and tucking it away in the fridge for fabulous roast potatoes – often enjoyed weeks after the last scrap of flavoursome meat has been devoured.

The big, boisterous and noisy birds are a major part of life in the Hickey household for several months a year. Helena says, 'We get them as day-old goslings in early July. At first they are kept warm, then they go out for a bit, becoming fully free range after a few weeks. It's lovely to hear them in the mornings, hooting as they go into the fields', she says. The birds grow up with the family, soon learning the routine of daily life. It's funny to see them practically walking themselves off to their field each day, to graze in lush pastures by the Atlantic, enjoy the fresh sea air – and take in the grand view of the bay with its impressive landmark ochre-coloured castle, owned by a certain English actor. At night, the geese are brought in to retire in straw-bedded barns and fed extra rations of mixed grain, free from additives, antibiotics and growth promoters. It's not surprising they taste so good. Their quality is down to slow maturing. Domestic geese don't take kindly to intensive farming, requiring this sort of natural, free range existence to be happy, healthy – and eventually – good eating.

The Hickeys' farm is a family home too, with five children in residence. Helena's kitchen is naturally the hub of the house, warm and roomy, with a kettle always on the boil and a batch of warm scones on the big wooden table. She bakes her own bread as well. With a business to run and a family to look after, you wonder just how she does it all. But she has everything under control – and Eugene already has some of the older children lending a bit of a hand with the farming. 'They help him bring the geese in sometimes', says Helena.

Skeaghanore Duck And Geese Products

Whole ducks, duck breasts and duck legs in vacuum packs. Whole geese at Christmas.

One of the thrills of a West Cork Christmas for anyone who decides to buy a Hickey goose direct from the farm is the journey to pick up the bird. It's like getting the first present of the season, big, heavy and ready for the oven. It comes as a bit of loss, even to a hardened farmers' wife like Helena, to see the empty acres after the goose season has finished. But, like all farmers' wives before her, she takes the philosophical approach. 'We get used to hearing their noise, so of course it sounds quiet when they're gone. But we hope we've done the best job we can in rearing them to be as tasty as possible for our customers. And we know we'll have more back again the next year.'

With the success of the farm and the embryo interest of the Hickey children, it looks very likely that the family tradition of poultry production will carry on for a few more generations yet. That's a very heartening thought for duck and goose lovers. We can look forward to enjoying the Hickeys' fine birds for years to come.

Glorious Christmas Goose

Traditionally, in Ireland, a goose has potato stuffing. This fruity version with apricots, walnuts and Italian parma ham is lighter and balances the rich meat. It is cooked separately to crisp on top, and the bird stuffed with apples and lemon to flavour the juices. Prepare stuffing in advance, then cool completely and refrigerate.

Make stock in advance. Place goose giblets in a large pan with remaining ingredients. Cover with 1ltr/1¾pts water and bring to bubbling, skimming. Cover and simmer for 1 hour. Strain and return stock to pan, then bubble to reduce to about 600ml/1pt. Remove from heat. Cool and chill.

For the stuffing, heat oil and gently fry onion and garlic until soft but not browned. Add mushrooms and fry to soften slightly. Remove from heat and transfer to a bowl with ham, crumbs, apricots, nuts, citrus zests and juice and sage. Season well, then mix with beaten egg to bind. Spoon into a buttered ovenproof dish and dot with extra butter. Cover and chill until required. Remove from fridge 15 minutes before cooking.

SERVES 6

FOR THE STOCK:
- Goose giblets, rinsed and patted dry
- 1 onion, peeled and roughly chopped
- 1 carrot, peeled and roughly chopped
- 1 bay leaf and 3 sprigs parsley

FOR THE STUFFING:
- 2 tbsp oil
- 1 onion, peeled and finely chopped
- 3 fat cloves garlic, peeled and crushed
- 225g /8oz mushrooms, wiped and roughly chopped
- 100g/4oz wafer-thin parma ham slices, shredded
- 275g/10oz fresh white breadcrumbs
- 100g/4oz no-soak apricots, snipped
- 100g/4oz walnuts, chopped
- grated zest of an orange and lemon
- good squeeze of lemon juice
- 2 tbsp chopped sage
- sea salt and freshly ground black pepper
- beaten egg to bind
- butter for dotting

Wipe goose inside and out and prick the skin all over to allow fat to run during cooking. Season inside and out with sea salt and freshly ground black pepper. Weigh the bird and calculate cooking time at 15 minutes per 450g/1lb. Halve apples and lemon and place in the cavity. Sit the bird on a trivet in a large deep roasting tray and pop into a preheated oven, Gas 6/400°F/200°C for 20 minutes. Lower heat to Gas 4/350°F/180°C and cook for remaining cooking time, or until juices run clear when thick part of thigh is pierced with a skewer. Cover legs with foil if they are browning too quickly. Now and then, pour off the fat into a clean bowl. Remove cover from stuffing and place in oven for last 45 minutes or until browned, cooked through and slightly crisp on top.

When bird is ready, remove to a serving platter and leave to rest while making gravy. Pour off excess fat from roasting tray and add flour. Stir to scrape up any sediment. Gradually stir in wine and giblet stock. Bring to bubbling. Simmer for a couple of minutes. Season. Strain into a sauce boat.

Serve the goose decorated with fresh watercress, with gravy and stuffing separately.

FOR THE GOOSE AND GRAVY:
· 5kg/11lb oven-ready goose with giblets for stock recipe
· 2 dessert apples
· 1 lemon
· 1 tbsp sifted flour
· glass red wine
· watercress sprigs for decoration

Peppered Duck Breasts with Creamy Spinach

Duck breast fillets are convenient for this recipe, and just right when you want to make an impression for a special dinner. These are spiced with cracked black pepper, pressed all over the flesh, quickly sealed in a hot pan to brown, then oven finished until just pink in the middle. I like duck pink and juicy – but cook it longer if you must. Serve the breasts thickly sliced on some buttery, nutmeg-scented wilted baby spinach leaves turned in fresh cream, and mashed potatoes to soak up the juice.

SERVES 4

· 3 tbsp black peppercorns, cracked
· 4 duck breast fillets
· sea salt and freshly ground black pepper
· 50g/2oz butter
· 450g/1lb baby spinach leaves, rinsed and spin dried
· 150ml/¼pt cream
· good grating whole nutmeg

Press peppercorns into duck breasts all over. Heat a heavy bottomed frying pan over a high heat. Place duck breasts in skin side down, to brown. Turn over to brown other sides. Transfer to roasting tray and place in a preheated oven, Gas 6/400°F/200°C for about 8 minutes, depending on thickness, for pink duck, or until cooked to preference. When the duck is ready, remove from oven and keep warm, seasoning first with a little sea salt. Melt butter in a deep-sided pan or wok and add spinach leaves. Wilt over medium heat, then add cream, nutmeg and seasoning and stir to heat through. Spoon onto warmed plates. Slice duck breasts thickly and pop on top. Serve with mashed potatoes.

Duck with Olives and Almonds

Spanish-style duck stew with the piquancy of green olives and bone-dry fino sherry, enriched with ground almonds – delicious for a festive family gathering.

Heat oil in a pan and fry onion and garlic until softened. Remove and transfer to a deep flameproof casserole with a lid. Fry duck pieces to brown well all over and transfer to casserole. Pour over sherry and stock and bring to the boil. Lower heat, add herbs, cover and simmer for an hour or until duck is tender.

Stir almonds, cream and olives into casserole. Season with salt and freshly ground black pepper and lemon juice. Reheat to bubbling. Sprinkle in parsley before serving.

SERVES 4

· 2 tbsp oil
· 1 onion, peeled and finely chopped
· 2 cloves garlic, peeled and crushed
· 1 oven-ready duck, cut into 8 joints
· 1 wine glass fino sherry
· 600ml/1pt chicken or duck stock
· few sprigs thyme and a bayleaf
· 4 tbsp ground almonds
· 2 tbsp double cream
· 12 green olives
· salt and freshly ground black pepper
· squeeze of lemon
· 1 tbsp fresh chopped parsley

Risotto of Duck and Mushrooms

Intense winter flavours combine in this creamy risotto with field and wild mushrooms and fresh sage. If you can't get fresh ceps, use 50g/2oz dried and reconstitute in 150ml/¼pt water. Use this as part of the cooking liquid.

Fry duck pieces skin side down first in a heavy bottomed flameproof casserole until browned, then turn over to cook other sides. Remove from pan with a slotted spoon and reserve. If necessary, add a splash of oil to pan and cook onion and garlic gently until softened. Add mushrooms and cook for another minute. Return duck pieces to casserole with rice and stir for a minute so the grains soak up the flavours. Add a ladle of stock. Bubble, then simmer until absorbed. Add another ladle of stock, and continue like this, adding liquid gradually, simmering between additions until all is absorbed and rice is tender. The amount of stock varies, so keep an eye on the proceedings. Stir in sage leaves, butter and parmesan and season. Serve extra parmesan for sprinkling.

SERVES 4

· 2 large duck breast fillets, cut in cubes
· splash of sunflower oil
· 1 onion, peeled and finely chopped
· 2 cloves garlic, peeled and crushed
· 2 field mushrooms, wiped and sliced
· 2 wild ceps, wiped and sliced (or use dried, soaked as above, drained and patted dry)
· 275g/10oz arborio rice
· 850ml/1½pt chicken or duck stock (approx.)
· few fresh sage leaves, roughly chopped
· 25g/1oz butter
· 1 tbsp freshly grated parmesan
· salt and freshly ground black pepper
· extra grated parmesan for serving

Warm Duck and Noodle Salad

Duck has an affinity with oriental flavourings, made famous by the Crispy Duck served in Chinese restaurants. The rich dark meat is blessed by the presence of chilli, fresh ginger and garlic. That's certainly the case in this warm salad with its soy and sesame oil dressing. This makes a good first course or a light lunch.

Place duck breast fillets skin side down in a heavy bottomed frying pan over high heat and cook to brown skins. Turn over to brown other sides. Lower heat and cover to finish cooking for about 8 minutes until pink, or longer to preference. While duck is cooking, place noodles in a pan of boiling water, then remove from heat and leave for a couple of minutes until noodles are soft. Drain and drizzle with oil to stop them sticking together. Place in a large bowl. Remove duck from pan and slice thinly. Add to bowl with spring onions, beansprouts and pepper. Mix dressing ingredients and pour over. Add coriander and toss, then serve in a tumble on a platter or in separate bowls. Decorate with more coriander and chopped toasted peanuts if using.

SERVES 4 AS A FIRST COURSE,
2 FOR LUNCH

- 2 duck breast fillets
- 100g/4oz fine egg noodles
- sunflower oil for drizzling
- 6 spring onions, trimmed and cut into lengths
- 100g/4oz fresh, crisp beansprouts, rinsed and drained well
- 1 sweet red pepper, seeded and in matchstick strips
- 1 tbsp coriander leaves, torn
- 1 tbsp chopped toasted peanuts (optional), and extra coriander sprigs for decoration

FOR THE DRESSING:
- 1 tbsp soy sauce
- 1 red chilli, seeded and finely chopped
- 1 clove garlic, peeled and crushed
- 2 tbsp sunflower oil
- 2 tbsp sesame oil
- juice and grated zest of a lime

More Ideas for Fresh Duck and Goose

- After Christmas, the huge goose carcass makes delicious stock for a meaty soup. Simply strip off any remaining meat and dice into small chunks. Reserve these for the finished soup. Chop the carcass until the pieces are small enough to fit into a big pot. Add 1 chopped onion, 1 chopped leek, 2 chopped carrots, 2 unpeeled cloves garlic, 3 sticks celery, few black peppercorns, few parsley and thyme sprigs and cover with water (about 1.7ltr/3pt). Bring to bubbling then turn down heat to simmer. Skim the surface scum off. Simmer for at least an hour, topping up with more water if the levels dip down too much. (You need to end up with about 1.1l/2pt stock.) Strain and leave to cool so the fat layer settles on top. If the stock is chilled, the fat will make a solid layer which is easier to remove. For the soup, heat 2 tbsp oil in a pan and fry 1 peeled and finely chopped onion, with 2 peeled and crushed garlic cloves, 1 peeled and diced carrot, 2 sticks diced celery and a peeled and chopped potato. Pour over skimmed goose stock and bring to bubbling. Simmer until vegetables are tender. Add the reserved diced goose meat and season with salt and lots of freshly ground black pepper. Simmer for a few minutes more to heat everything through thoroughly. Sprinkle in 1 tbsp fresh finely chopped parsley.

- Goose fat roast potatoes are the ultimate – and one bird can provide enough fat to last until Easter! It keeps well in sealed jars in the fridge. For the best crackly potatoes, parboil the peeled chunks first, then drain and shake in the colander to roughen up the edges. Meanwhile, heat a couple of tablespoons of the goose fat in the roasting tray in a hot oven, Gas 5/375°F/190°C. Carefully place the potatoes in the hot fat, being careful that it doesn't spit. Turn the pieces to cover them with fat then return to oven to cook for 40 minutes or until golden and crisp outside and tender in the middle.

- Duck or goose crisps up better during roasting if the skin is pricked all over with the point of a small sharp knife, then rubbed with crunchy sea salt flakes. There is no need to pour any other fat on to the bird. It will give out its own fat as it cooks. Pour this off at intervals and reserve for the roast potatoes above.

Madeline McKeever – Organic Beef Farmer and Seed Saver

If there is one thing this country can't be beaten on, it's the quality of its beef. The Irish grass-fed system is one of the best in the world. Inclement weather means plenty of rain, making grass soft, lush and full of goodness. In summer, the country-side provides fresh grazing, and home-grown silage for the winter months.

In Skibbereen, West Cork, not far from Turk Head on the coast, Madeline McKeever farms organic beef on wind-swept land overlooking the Atlantic. Her small cottage points seaward, its stone front weathered by the storms and sea gales that have battered it over the years.

Madeline, originally from County Meath, studied and earned her degree in Botany at Trinity College, Dublin. It was much earlier than this though, in her secondary school years, that she first discovered an interest in farming, reading books borrowed from the personal collection of Christopher Fettes, initiator of the Irish Green Party, and a teacher at Madeline's secondary school. Later on, as a postgraduate, Madeline took off to the United States, enjoying a spell on an organic farm there, where traditional methods were employed to rear livestock. When she eventually came home to Ireland, with her then husband, the two settled in West Cork, started a family, and set up an organic dairy farm with just twelve cows.

Unfortunately the marriage ended, though Madeline's love for farming didn't. After her separation, she continued milking alone, facing the pressure of new hygiene regulations, which meant huge investment in the business to stay ahead. At the same time, as a single parent, Madeline struggled to cope with the demands of the farm and the responsibilities of a young family. She looks back now on those days, commenting that 'It was incredibly hard work, especially with small children.' Eventually, wanting to continue in farming, but unable to make the dairy business a viable economic option working alone, she took the decision to swap the cows for a small herd of traditional organic beef cattle. Now, Madeline looks after around 13 Hereford crosses of varying ages.

Her Ardagh Organic Beef, certified by the Irish Organic Trust, is sourced from approved organic Irish herds.

Madeline rears her animals from the weanling stage, preferring calves that have remained suckling with their mothers until 6 months of age. For the young animals, early days on the farm are spent indoors, getting used to their new surroundings. Once settled, they go out to graze with the rest of the herd, enjoying a diet of organic fresh grass from pastures wetted by the morning mist off the Atlantic Ocean in summer, and the farm's own organic silage supplemented with a little organic barley in winter. Madeline prefers heifers, which are ready at about 18 months of age, and produce tender, tasty beef.

For the finishing process, Madeline looks to a local butcher who arranges slaughter and dresses the carcasses. Her beef is hung for at least two weeks, to allow the flesh to tenderize, and the flavour to develop into intense, satisfying beefiness. 'I sell the meat frozen in pre-cut portions direct from the farm', she says.

Madeline's beef loses none of its flavour or moisture after defrosting or during cooking. Because of the natural diet, and lack of growth promoters or antibiotics,

the meat has a generous marbling of fat encasing and running through the flesh. This is one of the best signs of good quality Irish beef and absolutely vital for optimum taste and texture, ensuring succulent meat after cooking. Madeline slaughters her animals one at a time, issuing an emailed newsletter to let regular purchasers know when each is ready for sale, advising on which cuts are available, and how long they have been hung. Quite often, some cuts are already spoken for long before the letter reaches her many ready and waiting customers.

Ardagh Beef Buys

Fillet beef,
striploin steak,
sirloin steak,
round steak and roast beef joints,
stewing beef,
mince,
whole sides of beef available,
Cattle Dogs (Madeline's own
beef sausages).

Ardagh Organic Beef striploin steak is beautifully succulent, juicy and needs nothing more than a smear of garlic before grilling or pan frying until browned on the outside and pink in the centre. The dark, flavoursome, stewing beef is essential for a hearty 'Beef and stout pie', giving its richness to the gravy, as it cooks beneath a golden puff pastry crust. Familiar cuts, such as round steak slices or joints for roasting, mince, and meaty sirloin steak are also available. A mixed box is a popular choice. And if the freezer's big enough, some customers choose to purchase Ardagh beef by the side.

As a Botany graduate, Madeline's knowledge of plants has led to her latest venture – Brown Envelope Seeds. As well as the beef, she produces and supplies seeds of vegetables, including traditional Irish and European varieties not grown for many years. 'I grow unusual veggies then save their seeds. I also get given organic seeds as presents or whenever people travel abroad. I grow the vegetables, then add their seeds to my collection.' This traditional practice of seed saving has been responsible for the reintroduction of many old-fashioned vegetables that have long since died out in commercial production. Madeline's collection so far has included Soraya, an Eastern European lettuce, Asparagus Lettuce, so named for its pointy leaves, and the chunky Green Sausage Tomatoes which look like small pale green gherkins, but have soft, intense tomato flavours. As an active member of the Irish Seed Savers Association, Madeline is extremely enthusiastic about the types of fruit and vegetables available from the organization.

'They have a good selection of indigenous varieties like the Irish Peach, which is in fact an apple, and Irish Molly, another old apple variety which would be well remembered in Cork. As the only registered producer of vegetable seeds in Ireland, organic or otherwise, apart from ISSA, I decided that rather than duplicate what they do, I would concentrate on producing seeds of varieties that do well here, not just ones from

the past, but also relatively modern ones. Many seed companies are removing ordinary open-pollinated varieties from their catalogues and replacing them with hybrids, so these others may become lost. The good part about globalization is that we have access to wonderful vegetables from all over the world. The goal of Brown Envelope Seeds is to enable people to grow their own food.'

As a small-holder, the politics surrounding agricultural issues today is something also very dear to Madeline's heart. She has huge involvement in local Green Party activities and, alongside the farming and seed saving, even found the energy and enthusiasm to mount a campaign and stand for local election in the summer of 2004. Madeline is also a fierce campaigner for market rights, having regularly sold her produce from a stall at various markets – and occasionally not without consequences!

'In August 2003 I was arrested, along with another market trader Quentin Gargan, for trading on Main Street Skibbereen. It took till July 2005 for the charges against us, under the Casual Trading Act, to be dropped, and we were given the Probation Act under the Road Traffic Act for obstructing the traffic. We appealed that decision in June 2006, our appeal was upheld. Our legal victory was based on the fact that Market Rights exist in Skibbereen and have never been extinguished. We campaigned in April 2006 to see that market rights around the country were exercised before they self-extinguished.'

Farming, in anybody's terms, is not the easiest occupation in the world, and certainly not for a female. But this female is no ordinary lady. Madeline McKeever is committed to producing the highest quality meat on a small scale. Her beef speaks for itself in the eating. Its juiciness, tenderness, flavour and texture prove what an almighty difference dedication makes to the end product. Because of her seed-saving endeavours, it is likely that many traditional vegetables, which may otherwise have been left to die out, and unusual ones newly discovered from far-off places, will now be protected, grown and, hopefully, in the future, enjoyed as part of an everyday meal. The recent and extremely successful McKeever–Gargan campaign to exercise market rights, which received much national press coverage, has ensured the re-establishment and use of those rights for many small towns and villages all over Ireland, protecting market traditions for years to come. The saying goes that if you want something done, ask a busy woman. Listening to Madeline's story, you can't help but feel the sentiment behind those words was invented for her.

Ardagh Beef Pie with Irish Stout

The intense flavour of organic beef is complemented by the sweet smoothness of Irish stout in the gravy of this beautiful, warming pie. It's the sort of dish you feel like eating on a cold Saturday evening in late autumn, when it's been raining all day. Good quality ready-made puff pastry is now available fresh and frozen from supermarkets, cutting out time spent on lengthy preparation at home. Make the most of the convenience and use ready-made puff for topping this pie. Whilst I would usually advocate that food which takes time and care to make is ultimately always worth the effort, even I cheat on this one!

For the filling, heat 1 tbsp oil in a pan and fry onion and garlic until soft but not browned. Remove from pan and transfer to a heavy bottomed deep saucepan with a lid. Add a little more oil and fry the carrot, celery and mushrooms to soften slightly. Add these to saucepan. Next, coat the beef in seasoned flour and dust off excess. Add another splash of oil to frying pan, heat it until smoking, then fry beef in batches to brown well. As each batch is ready, transfer it to the vegetables in the pan. When all is cooked and in the saucepan, stir in tomato puree, then pour over the stout and stock, and bring to bubbling, stirring. Season and add herbs. Cover with the lid, and cook at the lowest possible simmer, for 2 hours, or until meat is very tender. Keep an eye on liquid levels and top up with extra stock if necessary. Remove from heat and cool. Transfer to an ovenproof pie dish.

SERVES 4

· 3 tbsp sunflower oil (approx.)
· 1 onion, peeled and finely chopped
· 2 cloves garlic, peeled and crushed
· 1 carrot, peeled and chopped
· 2 sticks celery with leaves, trimmed and chopped
· 2 field mushrooms, wiped and sliced
· 900g/2lb organic stewing beef, in chunks
· seasoned flour for dipping
· 1 tbsp tomato puree
· 150ml/¼pt Irish stout
· 600ml/1pt beef stock
· sea salt and freshly ground black pepper
· 1 bay leaf
· 2 tsp fresh chopped thyme leaves
· 1 tbsp finely chopped fresh parsley
· 350g/12oz pack puff pastry, defrosted if frozen
· beaten egg for glazing

Roll out pastry on a lightly floured worktop and cut piece to fit the top of the pie dish. Cut a strip from remaining pastry to fit the rim of the dish. Lay the pastry strip round the rim, pressing it down, then dampen it with a little water. Put the pastry lid on top, pressing it down on to the rim of the dish, and crimping edges to seal. Make a tiny hole in the centre to allow the steam to escape. Brush well with beaten egg to give a shiny golden glaze after cooking. Use pastry trimmings to make leaf decorations for the pie crust, if you like. Attach these with beaten egg, then brush them to glaze.

Preheat oven to Gas 6/400°F/200°C. Cook pie for 25 minutes or until crust is golden and risen and filling is piping hot. Some cooked cabbage and a bowl of steamed potatoes are perfect accompaniments.

Mustard Roast Beef and Yorkshire Puddings

I come from Yorkshire, so Yorkshire pudding was part of our very existence – served not just with beef, but any Sunday roast, otherwise a war would start! It's the same in my own home today. In bygone days, Yorkshire puds were always served first with the beef gravy, as a filler, to make a small joint of meat stretch further. We often observed this tradition, simply because we loved the pudding so much we'd have been happy to have just that. My mother always made her pudding in a big tray then cut it into squares for serving. Nowadays though, it's trendier to make it in little patty tins, to give individual, round, puffed-up puddings that are served together with the beef and veggies. Some chefs even make teeny puds, then fill them with rare roast beef and horseradish as posh canapés. I don't know what any of my long-gone Yorkshire born and bred ancestors would have made of that. The method of making the pudding is my own – slightly different to the way I was taught as a child, but it works very well indeed.

Place beef in a roasting tray, and brush all over with oil. Season with freshly ground black pepper and smear with crushed garlic and mustard. Roast at Gas 5/375°F/190°C for 15 minutes per 450g/1lb plus 15 minutes for medium meat, a little longer for well-done beef.

For the puddings, place eggs in a bowl with a little of the milk and water mix. Whisk together until frothy. Gradually beat in sifted flour with salt, whisking all the time until a thick smooth batter is obtained. Thin it out by gradually adding the remaining milk and water, whisking well between additions. Leave to stand for 10 minutes. Pour a little oil into the moulds of a patty tin. When the meat is ready, remove it from the oven to rest, then turn up the oven to Gas 7/425°F/220°C. Pop the patty tin in to heat the oil until smoking. Carefully lift out, then spoon some batter into each mould. It should sizzle as it hits the hot oil. Return to oven and cook for 20 minutes, or until golden and well risen.

To make gravy, remove meat from roasting tray and pour off excess fat, leaving just a tablespoon in the tray. Add flour and cook over medium heat for a minute. Stir in red wine gradually, then stock, and bring to bubbling. Simmer for a few minutes, season and strain. Serve the beef and puddings with roast potatoes, vegetables and gravy.

SERVES 4–6

· 1.8kg/4lb roasting joint of organic beef (rib, if available, is perfect)
· sunflower oil
· sea salt and freshly ground black pepper
· 2 cloves garlic, peeled and crushed
· 1 tbsp Dijon mustard

FOR THE PUDDINGS:
· 2 free range eggs
· 300ml/½pt milk and water mixed
· 100g/4oz plain flour, sifted
· pinch of salt

FOR THE GRAVY:
· 1 tbsp plain flour
· wine glass red wine
· 150ml/¼pt beef stock

Striploin Steaks with Blue Cheese

This makes a fine dish for the weekend. The blue cheese choice is up to you. Home-produced Cashel Blue or Crozier are both gorgeous. But if you like something from abroad, you might try piquant Roquefort from France, or the elite of English blues, Stilton. Serve this with thin French beans, cooked then tossed in a little butter with quartered tomatoes, until the tomatoes go squishy, and some new potatoes

SERVES 4

· 4 organic striploin steaks
· sunflower oil
· sea salt and freshly ground black pepper
· 100g/4oz blue cheese, crumbled

Heat a griddle pan until smoking. Brush steaks all over with oil, and season generously with freshly ground black pepper. Leave the salt until the steaks are cooked, otherwise it encourages the juices to run from the meat during griddling. Cook steaks until browned and char griddled one side, then turn over. A medium rare steak takes about 6–8 minutes depending on thickness. The steaks are just medium when little spots of blood start to prick the surface of the meat, and the steak still has a little give when prodded. Season with a little salt, then crumble cheese on top and leave for a moment to melt. Serve immediately.

Real Spaghetti Bolognese

Years ago, I worked with an English-born lady of Italian extraction – a very good cook as most who have been brought up in an Italian family usually are. The lady in question made the most wonderful 'ragu' – the meat sauce poured over spaghetti that is now commonly known as 'bolognese' – and always used a little chopped fresh chicken liver in the mix. Chicken livers are available in most good butchers. They give enveloping richness and sensuous moistness to this ragu – despite their humble price tag. For this particular recipe, I use all minced beef, though in Italy, it could be a half and half mix of minced beef and pork. I also include a little chopped streaky bacon which substitutes for Italian pancetta – chopped pieces of cured pork belly. Elizabeth David, in her book *Italian Food*, also states that milk or cream is sometimes added for 'smoothness'. I prefer it without – but if you want to add a generous splash of either, feel free.

Prepare chicken livers by washing, patting dry and removing any tubes or greeny bits. Chop small and reserve. Heat oil in a large deep saucepan and fry bacon with vegetables until softened and bacon is browned. Remove from pan and reserve. Add a little more oil to pan and the beef and livers, cooking in batches if necessary, until sealed and brown.

Return vegetables to pan. Add wine with chopped tomatoes, tomato puree and stock. Bring to bubbling, then turn down heat to very low, and cook for at least an hour (the Italians leave it cooking very gently for anything up to 3 hours) until the flavour is very rich and concentrated, adding more stock if necessary to keep it all moistened. Season and stir in oregano and parsley. Serve stirred through hot spaghetti, with some freshly grated parmesan to sprinkle on top.

SERVES 4

- 100g/4oz fresh chicken livers, washed and picked over
- 2 tbsp olive oil
- 2 rashers streaky bacon, rinded and chopped
- 1 onion, peeled and finely chopped
- 2 cloves garlic, peeled and crushed
- 2 sticks celery, rinsed and finely chopped
- 1 carrot, peeled and finely chopped
- 350g/12oz organic minced beef
- 1 glass dry white wine
- 400g can chopped tomatoes
- 2 tbsp tomato puree
- 300ml/½pt beef stock
- sea salt and freshly ground black pepper
- 1 tbsp freshly chopped oregano
- 1 tbsp freshly chopped parsley
- freshly grated parmesan cheese for serving

Boeuf en Croute

This classic beef fillet dish is just right for a big impression at a supper party. The glazed, golden pastry enclosing the succulent, tender beef fillet, first spread with a fragrant mix of wild and field mushrooms, garlic, Dijon mustard and parsley, is enough to bring everyone to the table. It makes a great festive treat too – either in the run-up to the big day or afterwards when everyone is fed up with the turkey.

Heat 1 tbsp oil in a pan until smoking, then sear the beef to brown all over, even the ends. Remove and cool.

For the mushroom mix, heat remaining oil in a clean pan and fry shallots and garlic until soft but not browned. Add mushrooms and cook gently, stirring, until softened too. Stir in mustard, lemon and chopped parsley. Season generously. Remove from pan and cool.

Roll out pastry thinly on a floured board, to make a rectangle large enough to wrap the beef. Smear half the mushroom mix down the middle of the pastry. Season beef all over, then sit it on the pastry over the mushroom mix. Smear beef with remaining mushroom mix. Bring pastry over meat to enclose, sealing down the centre, trimming off any excess. It must be a snug wrap. Seal all edges with beaten egg. Transfer to a baking tray, seal side down. Use trimmings to make decorations like leaves. Brush pastry all over with beaten egg. Attach decorations and brush these too. Place in a preheated oven, Gas 6/400°F/200°C for 25 minutes or until pastry is golden. The meat will be medium inside, so if you prefer it well done, leave a little longer, covering the pastry with foil to prevent over browning.

SERVES 4

· 3 tbsp sunflower oil
· 900g/2lb organic beef fillet, in one piece
· 4 shallots, peeled and finely chopped
· 2 cloves garlic, peeled and crushed
· 2 field mushrooms, wiped and finely chopped
· 100g/4oz fresh wild mushrooms (oyster, shiitaki, ceps) wiped and finely chopped
· 1 tbsp Dijon mustard
· good squeeze lemon juice
· 1 tbsp finely chopped fresh parsley
· sea salt and freshly ground black pepper
· 450g/1lb ready-made puff pastry, defrosted if frozen
· beaten egg to glaze

More Ideas for Organic Beef

- Horseradish grows prolifically in the wild, and in any garden. In fact, anyone who's ever had a horseradish plant in the garden knows what a devil it is to get rid of, if needs be. It grows like a weed, multiplying in size with every year. Horseradish sauce, the perfect accompaniment to roast beef, is made by grating the edible long pointy roots that grow below the surface of the soil, and resemble parsnips. You can sometimes pick up fresh horseradish in farmer's markets, or if you know a keen gardener who has some, try and beg a root or two from them to plant. That way you'll have constant supply, but you'd better be absolutely sure you want it before you plant it! To make this creamy horseradish sauce, finely grate 75g/3oz peeled horseradish and stir into 300ml/½pt lightly whipped cream. Add the juice of half a lemon, a good pinch of sugar and season to taste. Stir in some fresh finely chopped parsley. This makes a good accompaniment to mackerel too, in which case some chopped dill can be used instead of the parsley.

- Home-made beef burgers are a far cry from anything you get from a freezer packet. They can be customized to taste too, with the addition of fresh chilli for a spicy kick, wild mushrooms for a grown-up twist, or pieces of chopped sundried tomatoes, anchovy fillets and chopped rosemary to give a Provençal taste. This is the basic mixture. After that, do what you will. For four quarter pounders, place 450g/1lb organic minced beef in a bowl. Add 2 tbsp grated onion, 2 cloves crushed garlic, 1 tbsp finely chopped parsley and season with sea salt and freshly ground black pepper and squeeze of lemon. Mix well then add a little beaten egg, just to bind. Form into four burgers of equal size and shape. Cook under the grill or on the barbecue or shallow fry, then serve in crispy buns with lettuce, tomato and onion slices and pickles.

- Like the burgers above, meatballs rely on good quality meat to be anywhere near what they should be. I like to add some chopped fatty streaky bacon to the mix, to give it that much-needed moisture when cooking. Mix 450g/1lb Ardagh mince with 2 rashers rinded and finely chopped streaky bacon, 1 tbsp grated onion, 1 clove peeled and crushed garlic, 1 tbsp fresh snipped chives, 2 tbsp fresh white breadcrumbs, grated zest of a lemon, squeeze of lemon juice and seasoning. Mix together, then add enough beaten egg to bind. Nip off pieces and roll in to walnut-sized balls between floured hands. Chill for 30 minutes. Heat a little sunflower oil in a shallow pan and brown the meatballs all over. Remove from pan and reserve. Make a sauce by adding a little more oil to the pan, then gently frying a finely chopped onion with 2 cloves crushed garlic until soft but not browned. Add 400g can chopped tomatoes and a squeeze of tomato puree. Bring to bubbling, then simmer for 5 minutes. Add meatballs to sauce, cover and cook very gently for 10 minutes, until meatballs are cooked through. Check seasoning and sprinkle with extra chives before serving with boiled rice. You can spice up the sauce by shaking in a few drops of Tabasco at the end of cooking.

Willie and Avril Allshire
– Free Range Pig Farmers

In the old days, before intensive farming took hold, pig farmers raised their small herds in a free range environment, allowing them to wander and forage as they pleased. The resulting meat was firm, deep pink fleshed and naturally fatty, roasting to moist and juicy crackling perfection. Modern times have seen a general downturn in this type of production, with more and more herds being reared indoors. But the news is good in Cork. Old-fashioned free range pork is back – and tasting better than ever.

Large-scale pig farming has given the industry a bad name in recent years. Much bad practice has been exposed, showing some livestock to have suffered a poor quality of life. In the worst cases, dense stocking has resulted in pigs being confined in large numbers within huge barns, often with little or no bedding, a serious shortage of space, and sows forced to give birth in constricting farrowing crates to avoid any loss of young ones through inadvertent squashing. Fast turnover has depended on short maturation times, creating flabby meat, dry from lack of fat, and free of any real personality. This sort of practice goes against every animal husbandry technique necessary for these sociable creatures, which need time to fatten, and space and freedom to forage in the meantime. Back several hundred years, pig keepers often left their charges in the forest, where they spent the summer and autumn snuffling out wild greenery, herbs and acorns. By late winter, they were happy, fat and ready for the eating.

In Rosscarbery, West Cork, Willie and Avril Allshire have gone right back to that premise to rear their Caherbeg free range herd of Saddleback-cross pigs as naturally as possible, without antibiotics and growth promoters. Their farm, situated amid rolling green fields near the coast, once enjoyed distant views of Owenahincha Strand, before the couple planted a protective bank of trees on the exposed south-westerly side to keep out winter storms. The trees, now matured into a tall and elegant backdrop for the garden, create a sheltered,

sunny aspect, despite stealing the view. Willie and Avril's home is a typical West Cork stone cottage, where they live with their two young sons. They gave up a conventional lifestyle – Willie had a nine to five business as a printer in Carrigaline – to come to what was once their holiday house and rear pigs. They started with just one or two, which soon became twenty. Now their land, divided into large paddocks, is home to around 200 porkers of differing ages, who have the freedom to wander and live happy lives. Sows have their babies naturally, in their own straw-bedded houses, and the tiny bonhams, pronounced bonavs, soon learn to scramble out of the way when mummy's tired. Within a matter of days, they are running alongside her in the paddocks.

Caherbeg Free Range Pork Products

Dry cure loin bacon rashers,
dry cure streaky bacon rashers,
dry cure ham,
dry cure collar bacon,
all in natural or smoked flavours.
Traditional sausages,
pork and onion sausages,
pork and onion burgers.

Rosscarbery Recipe Sausages:
Traditional,
traditional gluten free,
spicy tomato,
Cumberland.

It's quite obvious the pigs rule on this farm. They have chomped their way through ditches, leaving behind just a pile of stones, rooted under fences into the paddock next door and the odd adventurer has even been known to stray further afield. Willie sometimes finds himself having to repair the odd bit of damage to a perfectly trimmed garden hedge when that instinctive desire to rummage – and eat everything in sight – surfaces in one of his pigs. He feeds the herd a special, natural cereal-based diet complemented with vegetable scraps and, in early autumn, windfall apples from the family orchard out front. The two Allshire boys are very at ease with the pigs, stopping to stroke the odd nosy escapee who has wandered up the lane between the paddocks to see what's going on, and often volunteering to distribute vegetable titbits from a bucket to eager recipients. These pigs take a long time to mature, so the resulting meat builds up its natural fat layer and has a texture second to none. In the raw state, a piece of Caherbeg pork has a thick layer of creamy white fat under a dark gold rind, encasing the deep pinky-beige flesh. When it's roasted, the crackling is tooth-crunchingly satisfying, and the naturally sweet flavour that of a bygone age.

The garden of the Allshire's home spills with edibles, all grown and used by Avril, a keen cook. The conservatory greenhouse is home in summer to prolific tomato plants, a fruiting lemon tree and mature grapevine, laden with big bunches of white grapes. As she stands beneath it chatting, one or other of her young sons will keep hopping up to grab a handful of the ripe fruits, before sloping off to munch them in the sun. Outside, the orchard has several varieties of apples and plums, bordered by hedgerow brambles where wild raspberries and blackberries are there for the picking. An herb garden, to the front of the cottage, is a mass of greenery, some planted by the boys, and all of which they readily point out and identify. In the kitchen, this farmer's wife applies her cookery skills to creating new recipes using their quality meat, including an intoxicating 'pork cake' heaving with fruit, which has Caherbeg sausage meat as its base. The recipe has been received well and now looks set to take local shops by storm!

Willie oversees farm production right across the board. His expertise is utilized in every aspect, from good animal husbandry right through to end product. The salting and curing of pork for bacon is a traditional method of preservation first used by the pig farmers of centuries ago, who, without

refrigeration or freezing facilities, had to find ways to utilize and store every scrap of the carcass of a precious home-reared animal. That premise, and a real passion and appreciation of good food, led to the development of Willie's own special dry cure for bacon and hams using meat from his outdoor herd and no added water in its recipe. As a result, Caherbeg dry cure loin or streaky rashers cook pleasingly crisp under the grill or fried in just the smallest splash of sunflower oil. Dry cure streaky bacon chops, thick and succulent, make the perfect summer barbecue feast; moorishly flavoursome cooked outdoors on a hot summer's evening and enjoyed with crisp salad and crackly skinned jacket potatoes. The Allshire's dry cure hams and collar bacon joints are the cuts for traditionalists who love to have a piece of bacon on the go for sandwiches – or a wholesome and filling plate of bacon and cabbage at dinner.

Sausages are another speciality, with the farm producing two distinct and delicious ranges in a variety of flavours. Caherbeg Free Range Traditional sausages are the élite of good old-fashioned bangers, based on free range pork, seasoning and sometimes a little fresh onion for extra oomph. Rosscarbery Recipe Pork sausages have a good smattering of pepper, perfect for a famous Full Irish breakfast, and the Spicy Tomato, with their generous brush of chilli, are great for a warming winter casserole, cooked with meltingly soft onions, garlic, tomatoes and butter beans, or in an old-fashioned 'toad in the hole' where the sausages are set to bake amid a light and golden Yorkshire pudding batter. Squeezed out of the skins, they also make the most superb stuffing balls to garnish a roast chicken or turkey, lightened with breadcrumbs, sharpened with lemon zest and juice, then wrapped individually in rashers of dry cure streaky bacon before being placed around the roasting bird towards the end of cooking time.

Rosscarbery Cumberlands are the ones for a classic and timeless supper of bangers and mash, and enormously popular with UK-based customers. With an eye to health and special dietary requirements, the newest kid on this block is a traditionally seasoned gluten-free sausage.

Such is the excellence of the two ranges, the products have been the recipients of medal honours in recent years. In 2004, Caherbeg Traditional sausages received a Gold Award at London's Great Taste Awards, chosen from thousands of international entries in 180 categories. They went on to scoop the coveted Reserve Best Speciality Product in Ireland from the overall competition that year. The 2005 awards saw Gold for Rosscarbery Recipe sausages, whilst the Dry Cure Collar Bacon netted two silvers.

The Allshires' success is due in no small way to the careful rearing and husbandry of their free range herd, and certainly proves once and for all that pigs really must be as happy as that famous saying goes to produce the best meat. Thanks to Willie and Avril, great free range pork is back in a big way. Hurray say all of us.

Roast Loin of Free Range Pork with Cinnamon Apple Sauce

Superlative Sunday roast – this is mouthwateringly delicious and irresistible. The secret of good crackling is first to get the rind scored by the butcher – in straight lines kept very close together. Ask him also to chine the bone to help with carving later. Massaging the rind well with oil and crunchy sea salt, rubbing it deep into the score marks, will help it crackle during roasting. The cooking process should be started with a high oven, then turned down once the rind has begun to crisp, so the meat can cook at a moderate temperature and keep its moistness.

Rub pork rind with oil then salt, working well into the score marks. Season all over with black pepper. Rub the meat with garlic and rosemary. Calculate cooking time by weight at 25 minutes per 450g/1lb. Place in a roasting tray bones down (these act as a natural trivet) in a preheated oven at Gas 8/450°F/ 230°C for 20 minutes to get the crackling going. Turn down oven to Gas 4/350°F/180°C for the remaining cooking time. Baste with juices now and again.

Meanwhile, place apples in a pan with butter, cinnamon, sugar and a splash of water. Cook over medium high heat until apples are fluffy and softened. Add more sugar to taste if necessary – though it should still have a hint of tart bite. Remove from heat and reserve.

When pork is ready, remove to a serving platter to rest. This lets the juices settle back into the meat before carving. Drain off all but 1 tbsp fat from roasting tray. Place over medium heat and add flour. Cook for a minute then gradually add chicken stock, scraping up to incorporate the meaty juices. Bring to bubbling, stirring, to thicken. Strain into a warmed gravy boat. Serve the pork with flourishes of watercress, with gravy and apple sauce separately.

SERVES 4

· 1.4kg/3lb loin of free range pork on the bone, chined
· sunflower oil
· sea salt and freshly ground black pepper
· 2 cloves garlic, peeled and crushed
· 1 tbsp finely chopped fresh rosemary
· 1 tbsp flour
· 600ml/1pt chicken stock
· watercress for decoration

FOR THE APPLE SAUCE:

· 2 large cooking apples, peeled, cored and chopped
· 25g/1oz butter
· pinch of ground cinnamon
· 2 tbsp sugar, or to taste

Farmhouse Pork Steaks

Choose free range pork chops cut from a piece of loin for this quick and easy supper. Get the butcher to trim off the skin and bone, leaving a layer of the top fat to moisten the steaks during cooking. Mature cheddar cheese and grainy mustard make a pokey topping. Serve these on green beans tossed with olive oil and chives.

Mix cheese with wholegrain mustard. Heat sunflower oil in a large pan until smoking. Add pork steaks and cook to brown on one side. Turn steaks over and season. Spread cheesey mustard mix on top. Cook to brown other sides, then cover and cook through (5 minutes depending on thickness). Meanwhile, cook green beans in lightly salted water until tender. Drain. Drizzle over olive oil. Add chives and seasoning. Strew on a platter and sit pork steaks on top to serve.

SERVES 4

· 4 tbsp grated mature farmhouse cheddar
· 2 tsp wholegrain mustard
· sunflower oil for frying
· 4 Caherbeg free range pork loin steaks
· sea salt and freshly ground black pepper
· 225g/8oz fresh thin green beans, trimmed
· splash of extra virgin
· olive oil
· 1 tbsp snipped fresh chives

Toad in the Hole

As a child, this was one of my favourite after-school dinners. I still love it – as do my own family now. Good-quality sausages are the key, of course. Sometimes, when my mother made this, she would add half a peeled and grated onion to the mix, which prevents the batter billowing up as much as without, but gives a lovely, oniony taste. It's up to you.

SERVES 4

· 100g/4oz plain flour
· pinch of salt
· 2 eggs, beaten
· 300ml/½pt milk
· 8 Rosscarberry Recipe sausages
· sunflower oil

Sift flour and salt into a bowl and make a well in the centre. Add eggs, bringing the flour in with a whisk, incorporating it gradually. Whisk in the milk, to make the batter smooth.

Arrange sausages in a roasting tray and pour in 2 tbsp oil. Cook in a pre-heated oven, Gas 6/400°F/200°C for a few minutes, until oil is smoking and sausages are beginning to take colour. Carefully remove tin from oven. Pour in the batter mix, then return to oven and cook for 25 minutes, or until the batter is golden, risen and crisp and sausages are well browned.

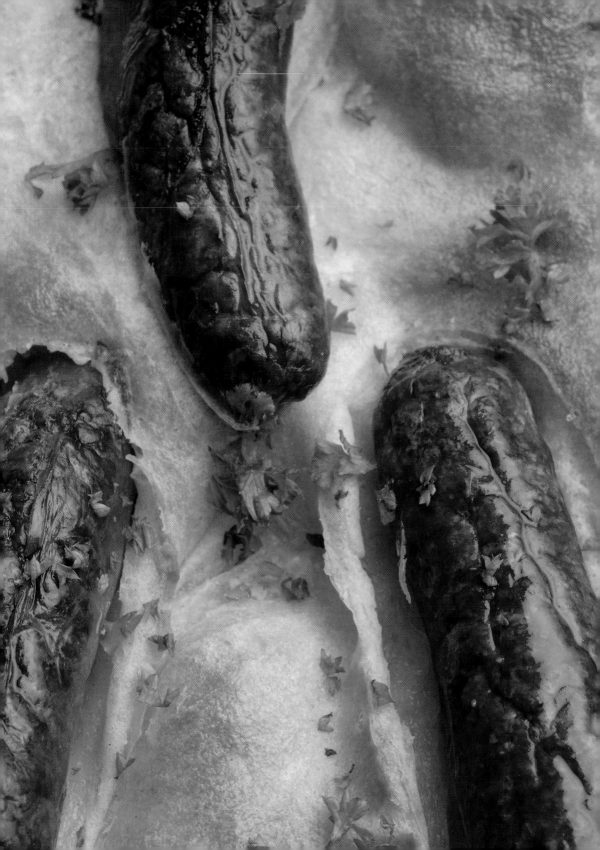

Hamburgers with Cucumber Pickle

Mixing best-quality pork with streaky bacon gives a lovely moistness to what could otherwise be a dry burger. The flavourings here lean towards the spicy, but the basic mix lends itself to personality changes in terms of taste. For a Mediterranean flavour, leave out the chilli and instead add a tablespoon of chopped black olives and 2 chopped anchovy fillets. For a winter supper, mix the meats with 100g/4oz chopped, and sautéed field mushrooms, and top the cooked burgers with a piquant blue cheese, such as Roquefort or Crozier. The cucumber pickle is another recipe I remember my mother making when I was small. It was always a Sunday tea thing with a salad and cold meat, but it's very good here.

For the pickle, place cucumber and onion in a dish and pour over vinegar. Add sugar and seasoning and cover. Leave to marinate for 2–3 hours or longer if you have time. This will keep covered in the fridge for a few days.

Mix pork and bacon in a bowl with garlic, onion, chilli and parsley. Season generously with salt and freshly ground black pepper. Add lemon juice and zest, and enough egg to bind. Work together with hands to mix well. Nip off a tiny piece, and fry quickly in a little hot oil to test for seasoning. Add more if necessary. Form remaining mix into four burgers. Brush with oil and grill for about 5 minutes each side depending on thickness. The flatter they are the quicker they cook, but chunky looks good. Top with grated cheese and pop back under grill to melt. Serve burgers on crunchy rolls topped with salad leaves, and slices of the pickled cucumber and onion. Tomato relish and mild mustard are also good.

SERVES 4

- 450g/1lb free range pork mince
- 100g/4oz streaky bacon, rinded and finely chopped
- 2 cloves garlic, peeled and crushed
- ½ onion, peeled and grated
- 1 red chilli, seeded and finely chopped
- 1 tbsp fresh finely chopped parsley
- sea salt and freshly ground black pepper
- juice and zest of half a lemon
- 1 egg, beaten, to bind
- sunflower oil for brushing
- 75g/3oz grated mature cheddar cheese
- crunchy rolls and salad leaves to serve

FOR THE CUCUMBER PICKLE:
- ½ cucumber, thinly sliced
- 1 onion, peeled and sliced in thin rings
- 150ml/¼pt malt vinegar
- 1 tbsp of sugar
- sea salt and freshly ground black pepper

Polpette

These little meatballs have an Italian name and flavour. They can be made in advance, rolled into balls, then left covered in the fridge to chill until ready to cook. The accompanying sauce is very easy and, again, can be made separately and warmed through thoroughly before the fried meatballs are added to finish cooking.

For the sauce, heat olive oil in a pan and fry onion and garlic very gently until softened and golden. Add chopped tomatoes and white wine and bring to bubbling. Add sugar. Simmer for 10 minutes or until reduced slightly. Season, add parsley and reserve.

Place pork in a bowl, with crumbs, grated onion, garlic, chopped herbs, almonds and lemon juice and zest. Season, then add beaten egg and mix well with hands to bind. Roll into walnut-sized balls. (Chill them for 30 minutes at this stage or, if made in advance, leave them in the fridge until ready to cook.) Heat olive oil in a pan, brown both sides in batches. Remove from pan. Add reserved tomato sauce to pan, stirring to scrape up any of the meatball cooking juices. Return meatballs to sauce and simmer gently for a further five minutes or until cooked through and sauce is slightly reduced. Sprinkle in extra chopped parsley. Check seasoning and serve with freshly cooked tagliatelle.

SERVES 4

FOR THE SAUCE:
· good splash olive oil
· 1 onion, peeled and finely chopped
· 2 cloves garlic, peeled and crushed
· 2 x 400g cans chopped tomatoes
· ½ glass white wine
· pinch of sugar
· sea salt and freshly ground black pepper
· 1 tbsp fresh finely chopped parsley

FOR THE MEATBALLS:
· 450g/1lb free range pork mince (it's worth asking the butcher to mince a piece specially for these)
· 2 tbsp fresh breadcrumbs
· 2 tbsp grated onion
· 2 cloves garlic, peeled and crushed
· 1 tbsp each finely chopped fresh parsley and rosemary
· 1 tbsp flaked almonds, roughly chopped
· zest and juice of half a lemon
· salt and freshly ground black pepper
· 1 egg, beaten
· extra chopped parsley to finish

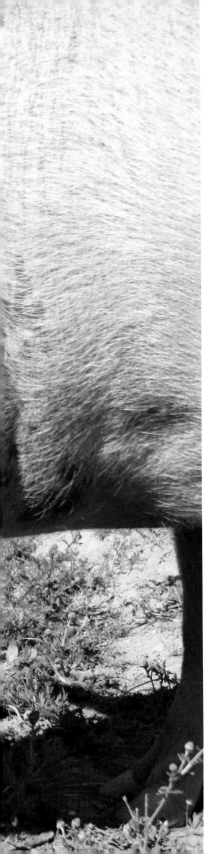

More Ideas for Free Range Pork

- A loin joint of free range pork is an excellent pot roasted with cider and leeks. For successful pot roasting, choose an ovenproof casserole with a tightly fitting lid that is just big enough to fit the joint of meat fairly snugly. To serve 4, heat 2 tbsp oil in a pan and fry 1 peeled and chopped onion, 2 cloves peeled and crushed garlic and 2 trimmed and sliced leeks, until soft and slightly caramelized. Transfer vegetables to ovenproof casserole. Heat another splash of oil in the frying pan and brown a 1.4kg/3lb joint of boned and rolled pork loin all over. Sit on top of vegetables in casserole. Add 150ml/¼pt dry cider and 150ml/¼pt chicken stock to pan and stir to scrape up sediment. Bring to bubbling then pour over pork and vegetables. Season, scatter rosemary sprigs over and around pork. Cover and place in a preheated oven, Gas 4/350°F/180°C for 2 hours or until pork is tender. When meat is ready, lift it out of casserole to a warm plate, and surround with the veggies, lifting them out with a slotted spoon. Cover and keep hot. Pour cooking liquid into a pan and bubble rapidly to reduce slightly. Stir in 2 tbsp cream and season. Serve in a sauceboat with the meat and vegetables.

- A few chopped dry cure bacon rashers fried crisp are a great finish for a creamy celery or celeriac soup. Scatter the bacon pieces over the soup just before serving.

From the Waters

From the Waters

All that stretches beyond the ragged cliffs of the Mizen Head and its lighthouse are miles and miles of blue Atlantic Ocean. The famine boats of Ireland crossed that water many times during a mass exodus from the country of those searching out a new life in America. They saw it as a place which promised something more than rotting potato crops and little possibility of work. Some were right, achieving a better standard of living, then returning eventually to take their families with them to this new way of life. Others never arrived. The passage, costing a Prince's Ransom, often ended up being the last journey they ever made. It was a time of great sadness for many loved ones left behind.

Today the waters around the coast of Cork are busy with cargo and cruise ships, passenger ferries and pleasure sailing craft. In East Cork, the harbour town of Cobh bustles with tourists disembarking from some of the biggest cruise liners in operation, docked in the deep water quay in the heart of town. The biggest get the brass band treatment on their return to the sea. Travel west, and admire the selection of private yachts and sail boats that speckle the bays around the trendy villages of Kinsale, Baltimore, Glandore and Schull. In summer, regattas and sailing competitions are the order of the day – their dates marked on the calendar months in advance by sailors from all over the country, and the world.

Among all these are the people who use the water for their living. These are the fisherman of the region. Castletownbere in West Cork is one of the busiest fishing harbours in the country, landing a massive quantity of fish yearly. The quay here is home to trawlers that can spend weeks at sea, their interiors designed and decorated to hotel standards. Alongside them bob the few remaining local day boats, fished from the early hours of the morning to late at night, and coming back with the freshest catches imaginable to be sold at local auctions. Smaller still are the shrimpers and lobster boats which dot quieter waters round the shore . The men who man these craft are hardy sea salts well used to sitting in an open boat and getting a dousing from rain or waves in the course of a day's work.

Everything a fish lover could want comes from the waters around Cork county. Superb black sole, lemon sole, cod, haddock hake and bass, mackerel, wild Atlantic salmon, beautiful mussels and oysters, huge pink Dublin Bay Prawns. You name it – it's all here. The Creators in this chapter are reliant not just on the kindness of the ocean, but on their own abilities to make the most of its bounty – and put it on our plates.

Sally Barnes – Fish Smoker

*These days, top restaurants are well known for
their shining female chefs. Women are making
their mark behind the scenes too, with an increasing
number at the forefront of farming and cheese
making. One lady has been involved with the Irish
fishing industry – and particularly fish smoking –
for a good many years.*

For Sally Barnes, making superlative smoked wild Irish salmon is a way of life
– the force that drives her every day. The argument will always rage between
connoisseurs that wafer-thin, translucent amber slices of smoked wild salmon
win over those made from farmed fish any day. As a leading artisan producer of
top-quality smoked wild Irish fish, and one of only a couple of women in the
business in this country, Sally is bound to agree.

From a small stone outbuilding in the grounds of her old rambling farmhouse
in West Cork, Sally started the now internationally famous Woodcock Smokery.
She calls the stunning scenery and nearby coastline around the village of
Castletownshend home. The village has a cluster of houses and shops lining
a steep hill meandering down to the quayside and the grounds of the majestic
eighteenth-century Townshend Castle, which looks out over the waters of the
Atlantic. This part of the coast, with its unbridled beauty and tranquility, has
inspired Sally to create the best smoked fish from the wild stocks fished in its
surrounding waters. Her suppliers are local small-boat fishermen, who bring
the pick of the region's fish, particularly wild Atlantic salmon in season, to be
transformed into a highly acclaimed delicacy sought the world over.

The gravelly voiced Scot settled in West Cork with her partner, a fisherman,
over 30 years ago. Her first fish smoker was an old tea chest with a hole in the
bottom, set over a fire, and the fish were trout her husband caught during a day's
angling. It was, she says, 'by default', that she acquired a proper kiln, received
in settlement of a bad debt. Angling friends asked Sally to smoke their catches

– and the word spread. In the early 1990s, after studying salt and smoke as a traditional preserving method, harking back to centuries before the invention of fridge freezers, when food was smoked for preservation and storage, Sally became quite literally hooked, and started business in earnest. Her small and exclusive operation runs from a converted outbuilding beside the house, sheltering under the swaying branches of the towering, mature Norway Spruce standing proudly in the front garden. Woodcock's smokehouse, tiny but well proportioned, is equipped with special preparation tables, two kilns and a walk-in chill room.

'I only use wild salmon caught out at sea by a few commercial small-boat fishermen in Castletownshend', says Sally. Each summer, the salmon journey through the Atlantic back to the same Irish rivers where they were born, to breed again. The wild salmon fishing season, from 1 June to 31 July, allows some to be caught en route when they are in their prime, after spending at least one winter at feeding grounds way out at sea. Vigorous swimming in cold water against strong currents gives unique firmness of flesh to wild fish. Because of her

personal commitment to using only wild fish, Sally must be able to acquire all the stock she needs for a year in the short duration of the season.

The Woodcock technique employs dry salting, smoke from oak chips and generous helpings of patience. Sally explains, 'Smoking takes place at low temperatures over several hours, which doesn't cook the fish.' Like any culinary art, salmon smoking requires practical skill and an inherent intuition. Woodcock Smokery salmon fillets are smoked flat on wire racks inside the kiln. Sally explains the process, saying, 'It takes a minimum of 12–16 hours, and anything up to a couple of days if air humidity is high. We aim for the perfect balance between salt and smoke and time.' The texture and taste of Sally's finished product is one not easy to replicate. Her salmon has a seductive moistness and mild smokey flavours that enhance the premium flesh of wild fish.

Of course, Sally's business depends absolutely on consistent numbers of fish being caught locally during the short season. Falling wild salmon stocks throughout Europe are a huge concern, and she has seen Irish catches go down in 25 years from well over 240 fish per day per boat to around that for a whole season now. She says, 'No single factor is to blame. One major issue is water quality in our rivers and streams. Even 50 years ago, every river here had a run of salmon. Pollutants change the chemical smell of water and if the fish detect it, they don't come back, which affects breeding.'

One can't help wondering if over-fishing of stocks is also partly responsible for the reduced numbers of salmon caught in recent years. Sally thinks not, saying 'We certainly can't point the finger at our commercial small-boat fisherman. They use only 12m boats, and have fish quotas which get lower each year. During the season, they only fish four days a week, 12 hours per day in daylight, and they must stay within 6 miles of shore.'

While studying Oceanography, Sally spent time investigating the feeding patterns of fish. She points out that Norwegian boats are now travelling direct to feeding grounds far out to sea, to gather great quantities of the small shrimp-like krill that wild salmon eat. These are used to make pellets for Norway's intensive farmed salmon industry. Krill are small crustaceans with material in the shells which colours the flesh of farmed fish, reducing the use of artificial dyes. The depletion of natural food in this way has a serious effect on wild salmon stocks. The boats also take capelin, which, together with krill, is basic food for all other ocean dwellers, including Baleen whales.

Woodcock Smokery's Section

Wild smoked salmon – sliced packed or whole unsliced sides, smoked haddock fillets, smoked whole sprats, smoked mackerel fillets, smoked kippers.

As part of a programme to conserve artisan foods, Sally is proud to be involved with Slow Food Ireland, part of the international Slow Food movement with over 40,000 members, incorporating food producers, chefs, writers and enthusiasts. At Woodcock Smokery, she also welcomes students and chefs who come from all over the world to work beside her, learning the skill and art involved in making smoked fish of this quality, and partaking of her knowledge of fishing and oceanography. This ongoing education programme is just another way of getting the conservation message across to food professionals. Some of these students stay much longer than they intend, and end up becoming part of the extended 'working family' that includes Sally's own two daughters as well.

As well as salmon, Woodcock Smokery produces a selection of other wild fish. The range includes Irish mackerel fillets, kippers and teeny whole sprats you munch from head to tail. One extremely popular fish is the delicate, undyed smoked haddock, which takes on a lovely, natural pale golden hue to the flesh, from the cold smoking process. It's a far cry from the blisteringly bright topaz-coloured dyed haddock fillet often seen on the fishmonger's slab. Poach a piece of Woodcock's naturally smoked haddock in a little milk or fish stock, and lap up the deliciousness of the opaque, pearlescent flakes of flavourful fish, perhaps topped with a soft poached free range egg for the ultimate in fast and delicious suppers.

Sally's motivation and proactive approach to artisan production and related hygiene and safety standards for small producers have been monumental, and will continue to be so. It would be extremely hard to imagine the food industry of this county, and indeed this country, without her boundless enthusiasm and energy. Woodcock Smokery products have won accolades at The Great Taste Awards, London, and the Ballygowan Food Awards from the Irish Guild of Food Writers, for which she says she felt 'especially honoured'. Honoured is exactly what Sally deserves to be, for creating works of edible art from what the sea has to offer. Ireland's food arena would be a much sadder place without them.

Soufflé Omelette with Salmon and Goats' Cheese

A soufflé omelette is halfway between a soufflé and an omelette. The egg yolks and whites are separated, then the whites whisked and folded carefully into the beaten yolks to give a light, fluffy effect to the finished dish. This one is topped with wafer-thin slices of smoked salmon and some crumbled soft goats' cheese before serving.

SERVES TWO AS A LIGHT MEAL (OR ONLY ONE IF VERY HUNGRY)

· 3 medium free range eggs
· sea salt and freshly ground black pepper
· small knob of butter
· 4 thin slices smoked salmon, sliced in strips
· 50g/2oz soft goats' cheese, crumbled
· 1 tbsp fresh parsley, finely chopped

Separate eggs and beat yolks with 2 tbsp water and seasoning until thick and frothy. Whisk whites stiff and fold into yolks with a metal spoon, being careful not to knock the air out. Melt butter in a non-stick small frying pan or omelette pan over medium heat, and pour in mix. Cook gently until base is set and golden, lifting it at the edge with a palette knife to test it. Finish cooking the top under a preheated grill until just set. Scatter over salmon, goats' cheese and parsley. Flip over to cover and slide out of pan onto a warmed plate. Serve immediately.

Castletownshend Broth

This broth combines the savouriness of smoked haddock with the naturally sweet taste of sweetcorn kernels, and uses potato to give consistency. It can be served as a main course soup, because it has so much going for it in terms of flavour and texture.

Poach fish in stock. Lift out with a fish slice and reserve liquid for broth. Break fish into flakes. Heat butter and oil in a deep pan and fry onion gently until softened. Pour in reserved fish cooking liquid and add milk and potatoes. Bring to bubbling, then cover and turn down to simmer until potato is just tender. Add fish flakes and sweetcorn and season with lots of freshly ground black pepper, and salt if necessary. Simmer a couple more minutes to heat the fish through thoroughly. Sprinkle in parsley and serve immediately.

SERVES 4

· 350g/12oz skinless undyed smoked haddock fillet
· 600ml/1pt fish stock
· small knob of butter
· 1 tbsp oil
· 1 Spanish onion, peeled and finely chopped
· 600ml/1pt milk
· 2 medium potatoes, peeled and in smallish chunks
· 2 tbsp sweetcorn kernels, drained if canned
· sea salt and freshly ground black pepper
· 1 tbsp fresh parsley, finely chopped

Kippers with Lemon and Black Pepper Butter

The best kippers are small with delicate, sweet tasting flesh enhanced by subtle smokiness. They make a terrific breakfast, simply grilled with a little butter melted on top. But this zesty and spicy butter turns them into a light lunch or supper dish. The pepper should be cracked, rather than ground, to give a bit of crunchy texture. Do this by working the peppercorns in a pestle and mortar, till they are cracked in to smallish pieces. If you don't have a pestle and mortar, put the peppercorns in a small deep basin and grind them with the flat end of a heavy rolling pin. This dish is good with a rocket, red pepper and red onion salad.

Make the butter by blending it with the herbs, lemon zest, sea salt and cracked peppercorns in a bowl. Lay out a sheet of clingfilm on a clean worktop. Place the butter in the middle, then roll up tightly to form a sausage shape, squeezing it to make it plump. Seal the film at each end by twisting. Chill to firm up.

Grill kippers for about 3 minutes each side, till cooked through. While they are grilling, place rocket, peppers and onion in a bowl. Season and drizzle with olive oil and balsamic vinegar. Toss lightly. Pop kippers on warmed plates, and top with a pat of the chilled butter to melt on top. Tumble a little salad on the side of each plate. Serve with lots of brown soda bread and butter.

SERVES 4

- 8 kippers
- good couple of handfuls of fresh rocket
- 2 red peppers, seeded and in thin strips
- 1 red onion, peeled and thinly sliced
- sea salt and freshly ground black pepper
- extra virgin olive oil
- balsamic vinegar

FOR THE BUTTER:
- 100g/4oz unsalted butter, slightly softened
- 1 tbsp fresh snipped chives or finely chopped parsley
- finely grated zest of a lemon
- crunchy sea salt
- 2 tsp black peppercorns, cracked

Smoked Haddock Niçoise

I think natural, undyed smoked haddock works well in place of tinned tuna in a Niçoise-style salad. Eat this outdoors on a summer afternoon, with a chilled glass of Muscadet sur Lie from northern France. A match made in heaven!

Cook potatoes in lightly salted boiling water until just tender. Drain, run under cold water to cool completely, then drain again. At the same time, blanch the beans in salted boiling water until just tender but still with bite. Drain and run these under cold water. Drain again. Cut potatoes in half and place in a bowl with beans, onions, olives, and hard boiled eggs. Remove skin from haddock and break up flakes, feeling for any stray bones. Add to bowl. Shake dressing ingredients together and pour over. Toss to coat. Line a salad bowl or platter with iceberg lettuce leaves, and tumble the fish mix on top. Scatter over parsley before serving.

SERVES 4

· 450g/1lb small new potatoes, scrubbed
· 100g/4oz thin French beans
· 8 spring onions, trimmed and chopped into lengths
· 12 stoned black olives
· 4 hard boiled eggs, peeled and quartered
· 450g/1lb undyed smoked haddock fillet, poached and cooled
· iceberg lettuce leaves
· 1 tbsp fresh parsley, finely chopped

FOR THE DRESSING:
· 4 tbsp extra virgin olive oil
· 1 tbsp white wine vinegar
· 1 tsp Dijon mustard
· sea salt and freshly ground black pepper

Smoked Haddock Fishcakes

Mashed potatoes, cooked smoked haddock, and spring onions form the basis of these lovely fishcakes. For a crunchy outer coating, you can dust them with flour, egg and fresh breadcrumbs before cooking. Serve with a simple crème fraiche, caper and chive sauce which has a little piquancy to balance the fish. Make four large cakes, or if you want to serve these as a starter, form into eight smaller fishcakes.

Place fish, potatoes, spring onions, lemon zest, parsley and seasoning in a bowl and mix carefully. Form into fish cakes on a floured board. Chill for 30 minutes to firm up the cakes before cooking. Gently shallow fry in hot oil until golden both sides and thoroughly heated through. While fishcakes are cooking, mix crème fraiche, capers, gherkins, chives and season. Spoon into a serving pot. Lift fishcakes onto a warmed platter and serve with sauce and a little salad on the side.

SERVES 4

· 450g/1lb cooked skinless undyed smoked haddock, broken into flakes

· 275g/10oz cold mashed potato

· 6 spring onions, trimmed and finely chopped

· grated zest of a lemon

· 1 tbsp chopped fresh parsley

· sea salt and freshly ground black pepper

· oil for frying

· 300ml/½pt crème fraiche

· 1 tbsp brined capers, drained and finely chopped

· 4 pickled cocktail gherkins, drained and finely chopped

· 1 tbsp snipped fresh chives

More Ideas for Smoked Fish

- A small scoop of smoked salmon pâté always makes a gracious little first course, full of taste and impact, but still light enough to keep the appetite on the edge and get everyone in the mood for what's coming next. It also has the advantage of making a lazy cook look like she (or he) has spent hours in the kitchen, since it can be made in advance, and arranged on plates at the last minute, to look impressive. For a touch of sheer, decadent luxury, top the pâté with a spoonful of the jewel-like, glistening, amber-coloured salmon caviare, available from good fishmongers and delis. For four, place 175g/6oz roughly chopped smoked salmon in a processor and whiz until finely chopped. Add 100g/4oz cream cheese, 1 tbsp grated onion, and 2 tbsp fresh cream and blend until evenly mixed together and reasonably smooth. Add more cream if you want a softer consistency. Transfer to a bowl and season with freshly ground black pepper and sea salt if necessary. Stir in 1 tbsp chopped dill and a squeeze of lemon juice. Chill until required. To make this look good, make scoops of pâté, either with an ice cream scoop, or by moulding the pâté between two dessert spoons which have been dipped in warm water. Arrange scoops on four plates. If using, spoon a teaspoon of salmon caviare on each serving, then scatter over extra chopped dill. Decorate the scoops with extra smoked salmon strips, twirled over, if you don't use the caviar. Serve Melba toast on the side.

- Use smoked salmon to create a tray of stunning looking canapés to enjoy with drinks. Simply ripple small wafer thin slices on to bite-sized croutes made from white toast cut into rounds with a small plain-edged cutter. Finish some with a little soured cream, and lengths of fresh chives, some with a blob of black lumpfish roe balanced on top, and the remainder with lightly cooked fresh asparagus tips. Arrange in rows on a silver tray or large porcelain platter, and they'll look like they were made by a professional. Allow at least six pieces per head.

Cornie Bohane – Fisherman

A rain-lashed winter night spent on a fishing boat
out at sea is not many people's idea of heaven.
Fishing, for those whose livelihoods depend on it, is
in the blood. These days, although Ireland is washed
with plentiful waters, it's not a profession many Irish
men are willing to take on.

Cornie Bohane from Lough Hyne, Skibbereen, was brought up with fishing. His father fished to supplement the income from their small farm. When Mr Bohane Senior took to the sea in nearby Baltimore, heading out into the bay in his small punt, young Cornie went with him. They were times, now long gone, when a fisherman caught as much as his boat could hold, and sold what he didn't need to the villagers waiting eagerly for his return to the pier. No flashy motor cruisers or expensive yachts bobbing in the now internationally famous harbour. No fishing quotas. No Spanish trawlers taking their share from the locals. And certainly no Irish naval officers, jumping on board to check paperwork and legality. A simple, if not always easy existence, for those who embraced it.

Cornie recalls those days fondly. 'I remember going out in the punt with my father from when I was around six years old. He used a line and we caught mackerel and herring.' Needless to say, there was always a fine feast in the Bohane household after a successful day on the water. 'I loved going out, but never really thought about fishing as a career till much later on.'

As a young man, Cornie's fondness for the sea remained very much part of his life. He took a job at the now defunct boatyard in Baltimore, working on repairs and maintenance to fishing boats. Today, that boatyard lies derelict, the rusting remnants of some of its last vessels still housed inside the broken stone and corrugated metal cavity. It's a permanent reminder of what was once a hive of activity. Take a walk past the building on a quiet, sunny late autumn afternoon, when the last of the summer's tourists have long departed, and it's

almost possible to hear the banter that went on inside. The lively conversation of the men who worked there still echoes in the silence. A gentle onshore breeze seems to carry just the faintest sound of cheerful whistling, from those who went about the daily business of getting boats back out on the water, where they belonged.

'In those days, it was practically impossible to get a job on a fishing boat. But while I was at the boatyard, I was lucky enough to be offered a place as a crew member. Back then, the social life was great – and the pay was good. It must have been the lure of the money that attracted me!', he laughs.

That was the late 1970s and Cornie's been fishing ever since. In his time, he's experienced fantastic sunny days when the Atlantic was as calm as a millpond, and the fish practically hopped into the nets. Other times, especially in the years when he used to spend several days at a stretch out at sea, leaving his wife and young family back home, Cornie has seen dramatic weather changes. A thick fog might suddenly descend, or the boat be pelted by driving rain, wind and rolling waves. Not much fun when you're miles off the coast in the pitch black. Fishing is a high-risk job, no doubt about it. Cornie has known fellow fisherman who have been lost at sea, and when it happens, it hits not just their families, but the whole community to which they belong. He had his own brush with death some years ago, as a crew member on a boat fishing off The Old Head Of Kinsale:

'One foggy night, something must have happened to the radar. The water was calm. But the boat must have hit the underlying rocks in the thick fog and we went down. Luckily, she had a partner boat. They were 'pair fishing', with the net being towed between them. We were pulled out of the water and rescued by the other vessel. Everyone was okay, Thank God.'

He is philosophical though. 'Any trade can carry a risk of accident. In this job, you just don't spend too much time dwelling on it.'

For the past 14 years, Cornie has skippered *The Falcon of York* – one of the three inshore boats still operating in Baltimore. She's 55 ft long and bright scarlet, her cabin's exterior proudly emblazoned with her namesake – a striking crest of a gold falcon in flight. Cornie, with the help of one crewman, fishes 20 miles of coastline from Castletownbere to Galley Head, heading up to 12 miles out. It's rare he spends longer than two full days at sea, and that's in summer, when the weather is good and the days are long.

'On those trips, I'd leave at midnight on Monday, and be back in by dusk on Wednesday evening. Nowadays, modern boats have terrific facilities. I have radar, plotters, navigational and life saving equipment on board. And the Met office is superb for the long-range weather forecasts and information. There's less chance we'd get caught out. But it could happen. The sea is unpredictable. You have to assess for yourself whether you think it's safe to go out and do your job.'

Today's high-tech trawlers certainly have the accommodation, equipment and capacity to stay out fishing for days and, in some cases, weeks at a time. Their catches are kept in large holding tanks below decks, until the boats return to harbour. Cornie's vessel is small by comparison. Even on a two-day trip, he must take at least a ton and a half of ice on board to preserve his fish. Atlantic waters off this part of the Irish coast teem with some of the most prized species in the world. Undoubtedly though, the best and freshest come from inshore 'day' boats like Cornie's. In autumn and winter, he spends just the day at sea, leaving at first light and returning before it gets dark. The boat travels a few miles off before the first 'tow'. When the nets are eventually hauled aboard and emptied on deck, the fish must be sorted according to variety. 'We catch a mix of black sole, haddock, monkfish and so on. You just have to get in there with your hands and sort them out, then box and ice them immediately.'

It's hard work, but worth the effort. At fish auctions, like the one in Skibbereen where Cornie's fish are sold, those in the know arrive early to scoop the pick of the day's catch. The place is crawling with chefs from famous restaurants, and top fishmongers. Alan Hasset is one of them. An ex-fisherman himself, he sells everything, from traditional cod, ling and haddock to elegant turbot and brill, all of superlative freshness, much of it from Cornie Bohane's catch, from a stall at various farmers' markets.

During the summer, Cornie also works a small punt like the one he knew as a child. He takes this out into the quiet waters of the bay to catch brown shrimps that are plentiful during the season, from 15 August to the end of October. Pots are baited in the evening, then Cornie returns the next morning to retrieve their little captives. The sight of these small shellfish, fresh from the water, still alive, and jumping from their crates, is a gourmet's treat. All they need is minutes in boiling water, before cooling and eating straight from the shells, with some brown bread and butter. Not many things in the world come close to their taste. Surprisingly, West Cork's brown shrimps aren't favoured so well by the home market, and most end up being exported to Europe in the frozen state.

Cornie Bohane's Catch Of The Day

Haddock, monkfish, black sole, lemon sole, mackerel, prawns, brown shrimps in season. All sold at auction in Skibbereen.

Cornie has real concern for the survival of the industry, knowing the number of men going into fishing today is in rapid decline. Not many want to take on the hard work, the risks, or the commitment to spending their days outside in all weathers. But it doesn't surprise him. He has witnessed first hand the changes that have taken place in fishing since his own father began. Fuel prices have increased to the point where some boat owners have been forced to give up their vessels for good. Quotas have been introduced and, with them, massive reductions in catches for boats that once made as much in one day as they now make in a week. Cornie has also watched the industry he loves fall prey to the burgeoning onslaught of legal documentation and paperwork that is now part of every other walk of working life. Yes, it has spread to fishermen, who must fill in their own log book every day, and are subject to impromptu inspection from the Irish Navy whilst out at sea. A breach in practice can result in hefty fines, and even the loss of a boat and her equipment.

These changes will ultimately have enormous significance for the future of Ireland's fishing industry. Men like Cornie Bohane are national treasures, and should be treated as such – wrapped in cotton wool and preserved just like any other rare and valuable object. But he wouldn't thank you for doing that to him. As he ties *The Falcon of York* up at the end of another long working day, his eyes scan the twinkling lights of Baltimore Bay, and he breaks into a smile at the very suggestion. 'You know, I'd find it very difficult to leave the sea. On a lovely summer's morning, you can go out at dawn, with the seagulls following you, and leave all your cares behind. It's a great feeling. As if the world really is your oyster…'

Haddock in Thyme and Lemon Batter

As a child, I was always fascinated by the whole palaver of the cooking in our local fish and chip shop. This was a proper fish and chip shop, not one that sold kebabs, burgers and sausages too. You chose either cod or haddock, in crispy golden batter, with real chunky chips, not frozen. They used to make their own fishcakes from two big thick slices of potato sandwiched with a bit of flaked cooked fish in the middle, then dip the whole thing in the batter. You might get peas as well, if you were lucky. We had fish and chips some Saturday lunchtimes, as a treat. When I was around nine or ten, I was grown up enough in my mother's eyes to go and get them. I loved that job. The shop was really popular, so there was always a queue. While waiting, I'd peer through the glass front of the counter, and watch the male owner of the premises preparing the fresh fish fillets for cooking. One by one, he'd meticulously dip the pieces of fish in a stainless steel oblong tub of pale, creamy-coloured batter he'd made himself, swish them gently up and down to make sure they were all completely covered and, as he lifted them out, he'd run the length of each fillet along the edge of the tub to drain off the excess. Then, gripping each one firmly between thumb and forefinger at the tail end, he'd carefully lay them in the deep fat fryer, expertly letting go just before his skin touched the hot dripping. Yes, they cooked them in a vat of melted beef dripping, as was tradition at the time. Once the fish touched the hot fat, the fillets would sizzle immediately and you could see the batter crisping up before your eyes. Little bits of batter would always fly off into fryer, and these were called the 'scraps'. Oh, the joy of a few of those batter scraps sprinkled on your chips. I used to ask for them specially. This batter is the nearest thing to that of my childhood, but I've added some thyme and grated lemon zest to make it an altogether more grown-up affair.

SERVES 4

- 100g/4oz plain flour
- pinch of salt
- 1½ tsp baking powder
- cold water
- finely grated zest of a lemon
- 2 tsp fresh thyme leaves
- 4 portions haddock fillet
- seasoned flour for dusting

FOR THE BATTER:
Sift flour, salt and baking powder into a bowl. Make a well in the centre. Gradually add enough water to give the consistency of thickish pouring cream. Stir in the lemon zest and thyme leaves. Leave to stand while preparing the fish.

Wipe fillets with kitchen paper. Dust in seasoned flour, and shake off excess. Dip into the batter, one by one, making sure all the fish is coated. Deep fry in hot sunflower oil, until golden and crisp. Serve with chips.

Black Sole with Caper and Tomato Dressing

Black sole is also called Dover sole. Its firm white flesh makes it one of the finest of fish, needing very little to turn it into a feast for a king. In this recipe, the fish is grilled and served with a warm dressing, piquant with capers, diced tomato and lemon juice. One large black sole will give four fillets, two from each side.

Brush fillets with olive oil and season. Line a grill pan with foil and brush this lightly with olive oil. Lay fillets on grill pan and cook under a preheated grill until flesh is opaque and cooked through.

Mix dressing ingredients together and heat gently in a small saucepan. Pop fish fillets onto warmed serving plates, arranging them nicely in the centre. Drizzle with dressing and scatter over chives for decoration.

SERVES 4

· 8 black sole fillets
· olive oil
· sea salt and freshly ground black pepper
· snipped chives for decoration

FOR THE DRESSING:
· 8 tbsp olive oil
· 2 tomatoes, skinned, seeded and diced
· 1 tbsp capers, drained and chopped roughly
· juice of half a lemon

Spiced Potted Shrimps

You are lucky if you can get fresh shrimps to make this. I'd beg, steal or borrow to get my hands on some! To cook them from raw, simply plunge them into a large saucepan of boiling water then bring back to bubbling for just a few minutes, until all shrimps have turned pink. Stir them occasionally. Drain immediately and run under cold water to cool completely. Once cold, remove the shells by peeling off with fingers. There's no easy way, but the taste is worth the effort. If fresh shrimps are hard to come by, resort to frozen defrosted ones, or some best-quality cooked and peeled prawns instead.

Melt butter over low heat. Remove and cool slightly. Meanwhile, place shrimps in a bowl and add Tabasco sauce, nutmeg, seasoning and lemon juice. Toss to mix. Pack tightly into four little ramekins. Pour over melted butter, then chill until set. Serve with lots of brown bread and butter.

SERVES 4

· 100g/4oz unsalted butter (approx.)
· 350g/12oz cooked shrimps (shelled weight, defrosted if frozen)
· few drops of Tabasco sauce (to taste)
· good grating fresh nutmeg
· sea salt and freshly ground black pepper
· squeeze lemon juice

Lemon Sole Veronique

Lemon sole has delicate flesh, less firm than its more expensive cousin – but it can be just as delicious. It works well with subtle flavours. Veronique is a classic French dish for sole. The fish is cooked in white wine and stock, then finished with cream and peeled white grapes. The sauce can be thickened with a roux, but I prefer it without.

Lay fish fillets in a shallow pan. Season, sprinkle over chopped shallots and add a squeeze of lemon. Pour over wine and stock. Cover and poach gently over low heat until fish is just cooked and opaque. Remove from heat and lift fillets out of cooking liquid onto a warmed platter. Cover with buttered foil and keep warm while finishing the sauce. Make cooking liquid up to 300ml/½pt with extra fish stock. Transfer to a small saucepan. Bubble rapidly to reduce by a third. This concentrates the flavour. Add cream and most of the grapes, reserving some for decoration. Simmer again to heat through. Season. Arrange fish fillets on warmed plates. Spoon sauce and grapes over fish, and pop remaining grape halves around to make them look pretty. Scatter with parsley and serve immediately.

SERVES 4

· 8 lemon sole fillets
· sea salt and freshly ground black pepper
· 2 shallots, peeled and finely chopped
· squeeze of lemon
· 4 tbsp fish stock
· 4 tbsp dry white wine

FOR THE SAUCE:
· 200ml/7floz fish stock (approx.)
· 75ml/3floz thick pouring cream
· 75g/3oz white seedless grapes, skinned and halved
· 1 tbsp finely chopped fresh parsley

Grilled Mackerel with Chilli and Basil

Fresh mackerel is one of the oily fish family, packed with precious Omega 3 fatty acids to keep the heart healthy. Mackerel flesh is moist and rich, so herbs, spices, tart fruit or citrus juice work very well as flavouring.

SERVES 4

· 8 mackerel fillets
· sunflower oil
· juice of 2 limes
· 2 small red chillies, seeded and finely chopped (or less, to taste)
· sea salt and freshly ground black pepper
· 1 tbsp fresh basil leaves, finely shredded

Lay fish fillets on a foiled lined grill pan brushed with oil, then brush the fish lightly with a little extra oil. Sprinkle with lime juice and chopped chillies. Season. Place under preheated grill and cook for a few moments, until flesh is just turning opaque and flesh parts easily when prodded with the point of a knife. Remove from grill, carefully lift onto plates and scatter with basil before serving with salad and jacket potatoes topped with sour cream and chives.

More Ideas for Fresh Fish

- Whole mackerel are perfect for the barbecue. Slash whole, cleaned and gutted fish three times each side, without cutting right through. Brush lightly with olive oil and season with sea salt and freshly ground black pepper. Squeeze over lemon juice and scatter with a little crushed garlic if you like. Stuff cavities with fresh sprigs of rosemary or thyme then cook on hot barbecue coals until charred and browned on one side. Turn over to cook on other side. The fish is ready when the flesh comes away from the backbone easily when prodded with the point of a knife.

- You can make a fast version of tartare sauce with ready-made mayonnaise. For 4, place 150ml/¼pt mayonnaise in a bowl. Add 4 finely chopped baby gherkins, 2 tsp finely chopped capers, 1 tbsp each fresh finely chopped parsley and snipped chives and, if you have it, 1 tbsp cream. Season and stir together. It may need a little squeeze of lemon at this point. Chill until ready to serve.

- Monkfish is one of the most firm and meaty of white fish. The bonus of having no bones once filleted is the reason people who are otherwise squeamish about fish like it so much. Its texture is perfect for threading on kebab skewers. For 4 kebabs, you need about 700g/1½lb monkfish fillet, skinned and in reasonable-sized chunks – about 4 or 5 per skewer, depending on how big you cut them. Thread the chunks on the skewers alternately, with pieces of green pepper and onion wedges between. Sprinkle with lemon juice and olive oil. Cook under a conventional, preheated grill, or on the barbecue, turning during cooking. Drizzle with a little extra olive oil and sprinkle with fresh chopped dill or parsley after cooking.

Frank Hederman – Fish Smoker

It's hard to imagine a kitchen without the convenience of modern refrigeration. But time was when the only way of ensuring a good supply of fish and meat was by salting and smoking fresh produce to make it last. The oldest method of food preservation is now an art, practised perfectly by a home-grown Master Craftsman.

Cobh-born Frank Hederman has been smoking wild salmon at his Belvelly Smoke House, just outside the busy seaport town, since the early 1980s. As a child, he watched fishing boats coming in to Cobh harbour, landing their catches on the quay. 'There was one man, Don Donovan, a herring processor' says Frank, 'who could tell instinctively the weight and quality of the catch, and how much the fish would make at auction. He had a tremendous brain. I used to watch him in awe. It was a great environment, and I was sucked in by it.' These vivid memories served Frank well, stirring the very beginnings of his own involvement in the industry.

Belvelly is the country's only traditional smokehouse. As you drive off the cross-river ferry to Cobh and head round the coast, the faintest smell of smoke hangs in the air, giving the game away as to what exactly is going on just a little further up the road. Situated right on the water's edge, Belvelly Smoke House, named after the townland, stands in a courtyard setting on the site of Frank's childhood home. The newly renovated family house looks out over the oft-misted waters leading into Cork Harbour just round the headland. Many influential food people and celebrity chefs have visited the smokehouse, all looking to chat to the man who is now one of Cork's most famous artisan producers. When asked about how it happened that County Cork was the area

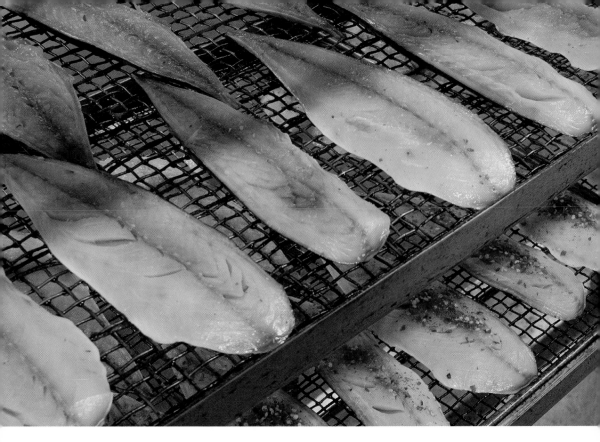

where many of the country's most prestigious and well-known artisans chose to start up, Frank says simply,

> 'It was pure coincidence. I suppose we were all looking for ways to diversify and make the most of natural Irish ingredients for premium products. Milleens, Gubbeen and Adrahan Farmhouse Cheeses, and me, we all got going without any of us really knowing about the others. Then suddenly, there was an artisan food movement here in Cork.'

Frank remembers those days only too well. Just after he started, three other smokeries sprang up in the area, set up by people put out of a job as a result of the closure of a meat factory in Midleton. 'Overnight I had three competitors', he says. As with all businesses, it's always the survival of the fittest, and Frank survived by going for the top end of the market and pursuing quality in all his ingredients. It's still his main objective today.

Ireland is known for its superlative wild salmon, spawned in rivers up and down the country and at its best for only a few short weeks in summer. Frank knows perfectly well the difference a dedicated fisherman can make to his end product. 'I only buy my stocks from the best coastal fisheries. They know the quality I want, and they mind the fish with care. It's very important the salmon are bled properly and not bruised before they reach me here at the smokehouse.' It's due in no small part to this attention at the hands of the men who catch the fish that Hederman Smoked Salmon is among the best in Ireland.

Salmon is cold smoked, so the fish is not cooked, just preserved in its raw state. Frank believes hanging the fillets in the smoker

Hederman's Hot and Cold Smoked Products

Smoked wild Irish salmon, smoked wild Irish eels (hot smoked), wild mackerel with various coatings like pepper, herbs (hot smoked), haddock (cold smoked), mussels (hot smoked).

provides the best results for his fish, giving a dryer finish to the flesh. 'Achieving the right proportions of salt and smoke is essential', he explains. Frank fillets and salts his fish with organic English sea salt, then smokes them for several hours, favouring small beech chippings, also from England. At one time, he used oak from the old whiskey barrels of Midleton Distillery. 'The quality of the smoke depends on the size of the chippings', he says.

Frank's smoking room, its walls black with tar, holds a treasure of golden fish, hanging on tenterhooks from the tenter bars attached to the ceiling. He built it himself, as a necessary upgrade to the one he started with – a free-standing 'cupboard'-style kiln where the fish hung from a single bar running across the top. It still stands in an outbuilding behind the smoke room, a significant reminder of simple beginnings.

When the smoke room is fully loaded with salted, filleted sides of salmon, the beech smoke is filtered in from the back. Originally, Frank piped it in from a small brick fireplace which slowly burnt the chippings he loaded in by hand. 'It took hours to smoke a batch of fish. I used to be able to sit there and read the *Irish Times* from cover to cover while I waited!' Eventually, the small burner was replaced with a purpose-built affair, which automatically feeds the correct amount of chippings into the fire in stages, then filters the smoke through at just the right quantity and temperature. Timings for salting and smoking can vary, according to the size of the fish. It's down to years of experience to judge exactly when each fillet is ready. After smoking, the amber-fleshed fish take on a moist texture and exquisite, delicate taste and fragrance.

Belvelly also produces cold smoked haddock fillets, and hot smoked local mackerel, mussels and eels from Westmeath. Hederman's fish grace the tables of some of the finest eating establishments in Ireland and England. TV chefs Richard Corrigan and Rick Stein are Frank's personal friends and regular customers. And diners at East Cork's Ballymaloe House Restaurant are well used to Frank's smoked salmon being part of the prestigious menu.

Frank Hederman remembers his earliest days of artisan prodction when, he says, 'it was a hard struggle for a long time'. Now he jokes of his 'overnight success – after 23 years!' But the fact is that, today, Hederman is at the helm of the profession, his fish sold in the smartest delis and food shops here and abroad. He is a member of Slow Food Ireland, and sits on the committee of the Cork Free Choice Consumer Group with other high-profile artisan producers and its Chairwoman Myrtle Allen. The saying goes that there is no smoke without fire. At Belvelly Smoke House, the flames are burning very bright indeed.

Smoked Salmon and Chive Eggs

Softest scrambled eggs with snipped chives stirred through, served alongside translucent, amber slivers of smoked salmon, make the most luxurious brekkie.

Beat eggs in a bowl with seasoning and chives. Melt butter in a non-stick pan. Add eggs and stir over medium heat, until the curds set softly. Remove from heat straight away, while they are still fairly runny. The heat of the pan will cook them more, but they should still be soft when served. Arrange the salmon slices in folds on the plates and spoon the eggs on the side. Serve with buttered brown toast, and lemon wedges for squeezing over the salmon.

SERVES 4

· 8 fresh free range eggs
· sea salt and freshly ground black pepper
· 2 tbsp snipped fresh chives
· small knob of butter
· 8–12 slices smoked salmon (depending on greed!)
· buttered brown toast and lemon wedges to serve

Fishy Penne

Sophisticated supper pasta dish which relies on great ingredients to be extra special. Smoked salmon really works well here, added just at the last minute and stirred through the hot creamy sauce. Try a glass of chilled Australian Chardonnay with this. Its own buttery creaminess is a super complement. And, if the weather is warm enough, this makes a lovely dish for an outdoor supper party, with a big bowl of organic baby leaf salad as a simple accompaniment.

Cook pasta in lightly salted boiling water until just tender. Fresh pasta takes only 3–4 minutes, dried takes about 12 minutes. Meanwhile, heat cream with cream cheese in a deep pan. Drain pasta, return to pan and pour over cream sauce. Stir through then add smoked salmon, reserving a few strips to finish the dish. Add herbs, lemon juice and plenty of freshly ground black pepper. Pile into bowls and serve immediately with remaining smoked salmon strips on top. Decorate with herb sprigs.

SERVES 4

· 350g/12oz penne pasta
· small pot fresh cream
· 1 tbsp cream cheese
· 225g/8oz smoked salmon slices, cut into strips
· 1 tbsp fresh herbs (chives, dill or parsley) chopped
· squeeze of lemon juice
· freshly ground black pepper
· fresh sprigs of herbs to decorate

Smoked Mussels with Fresh Cucumber Relish

Smoked mussels are heady with aroma and flavour and need only the biting foil and simplicity of this fresh cucumber and dill relish to complement them. Serve as a starter, with brown soda bread.

For the relish, peel and thinly slice the cucumber on a mandolin or in a processor. Place in a colander with salt and leave to drain for 30 minutes. Mix white wine vinegar with sugar in a pan over low heat. Bring to boiling and simmer for a few moments. Remove from heat and cool, then add dill. Rinse and pat cucumber slices dry and place in a clean bowl. Pour vinegar mix over and chill for an hour or so. Arrange mussels on little serving plates and spoon relish on the side. Decorate with fronds of dill. Serve with soda bread.

SERVES 4

· 1 crisp cucumber
· 1 tbsp sea salt
· 150ml/¼pt white wine vinegar
· 50g/2oz sugar
· 1 tbsp fresh dill, finely chopped
· 350g/12oz smoked mussels
· dill fronds for decoration
· brown soda bread for serving

Smoked Haddock Florentine

The word Florentine indicates the use of spinach in a dish, and this is one of my favourite ways of enjoying smoked haddock. The moist, poached fish, served on a buttery bed of wilted spinach leaves, with the oozy, creamy, extra-matured cheddar-enriched sauce poured over, is, in my view, a combo made in heaven. But don't take my word for it. Get in the kitchen and make it yourself. You can top it with a poached egg if you wish, but it doesn't absolutely need it.

SERVES 4

- 900g/1½lb undyed smoked haddock
- 25g/1oz butter
- 450g/1lb baby spinach leaves, rinsed well and drained

FOR THE SAUCE:
- 25g/1oz butter
- 25g/1oz plain flour
- 300ml/½pt milk
- 2 tbsp double cream (optional)
- 2 tbsp grated extra-mature cheddar, plus extra for topping
- sea salt and freshly ground black pepper

Poach the fish in enough water to cover. Reserve, keeping hot. While fish is cooking, make the sauce. Melt butter in a pan and stir in flour. Cook for a minute, stirring. Gradually add milk, stirring in each addition over low heat. Bring to bubbling and simmer, stirring all the time, until sauce thickens. Add cream, grated cheese and seasoning. Reserve, keeping sauce hot, and covering its surface with film to prevent skin forming.

Melt remaining butter in a pan and add baby spinach leaves. Stir around to wilt. Season. Spoon into a gratin dish. Pop drained hot fish fillets on top. Pour over sauce and scatter with a little extra grated cheese. Pop under a hot grill to brown on top.

Smoked Eel with Bacon and Baby Spinach

Frank's suggestion to eat his smoked eels with fried crispy bacon and a spinach salad is divine.

Heat oil in a pan and fry bacon rashers crisp. Blot dry on kitchen paper. Toss spinach in olive oil, balsamic vinegar and seasoning. Scatter in chopped spring onions. Tumble onto two plates. Top with a fillet of eel each then the crispy bacon rashers. Drizzle a little extra oil and balsamic vinegar around the plate.

SERVES 2

· sunflower oil for frying
· 4 streaky bacon rashers, rinded
· 100g/4oz baby spinach leaves, rinsed and spin dried or drained well
· good drizzle extra virgin olive oil
· few drops balsamic vinegar
· sea salt and freshly ground black pepper
· 4 spring onions, trimmed and finely chopped
· 2 hot smoked eel fillets
· extra olive oil and balsamic vinegar to finish

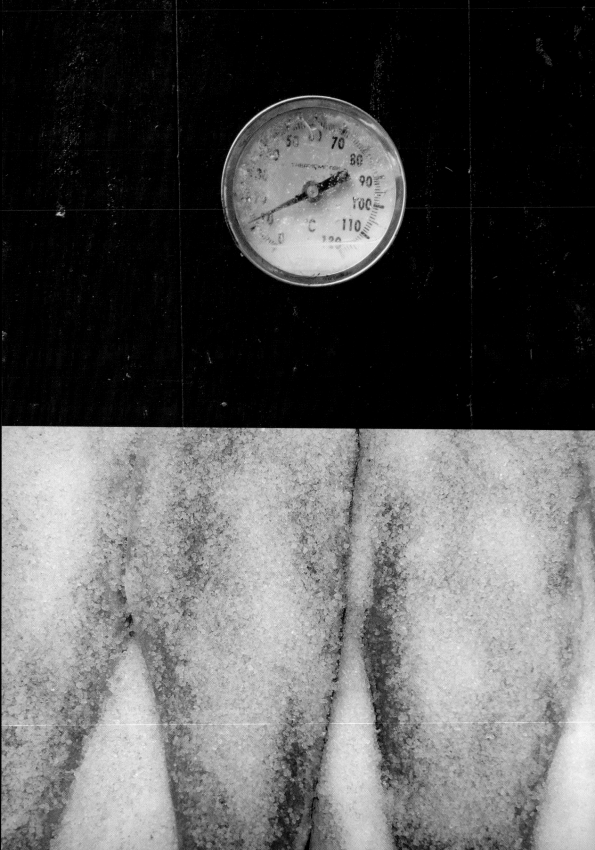

Other Ideas for Smoked Fish

- Rosti potatoes are a great accompaniment to smoked salmon for lazy Sunday brunch. For 4, peel and grate 3 large potatoes. Squeeze out the flesh in kitchen paper to extract excess moisture. Place in a bowl with 2 tbsp grated onion, sea salt, freshly ground black pepper, 2 tsp chopped thyme leaves, and 2 medium free range eggs, beaten. Mix together. Heat a splash of sunflower oil in a large heavy bottomed frying pan until smoking, or alternatively, heat a smooth-sided griddle. Place tablespoons of mix onto the pan or griddle, flatten down lightly, and cook until browned on one side. Turn over to cook other side. Remove and blot on kitchen paper. Cook in batches, and keep the cooked ones warm as you do the rest. Serve with a platter of sliced smoked salmon and a pot of sour cream mixed with fresh snipped chives.

- Smoked mackerel is excellent for a no-cook fish pâté. This one is easy peasy, and you don't even have to dirty the blender to make it. The fish is chopped by hand to give it lots of texture. For four, place 150g/5oz cream cheese in a bowl with a splash of milk and beat to soften. Skin 2–3 smoked mackerel fillets, 225g/8oz approx., and break up flesh, sifting through it with fingertips to detect any stray bones. Chop the fish into smallish bits by hand. Stir into cream cheese with 1 tbsp grated onion, juice of a lemon, 1 tbsp snipped fresh chives and freshly ground black pepper. Mix well. Spoon into a pot and chill. Serve on a platter surrounded with brown soda bread or thinly sliced toasted brown bread. If you're serving this as a first course, it looks pretty scooped onto individual plates, and decorated with fresh chives on top of each scoop.

- Smoked fish, like mackerel or salmon, add oomph to a salad made with leftover cooked pasta. Add some finely diced pepper, onion, tomato and cucumber too, then stir in enough crème fraiche or sour cream to bind the lot together. Season with freshly ground black pepper and sea salt.

Colin Whooley – Mussel Farmer

Roaring Water Bay. Its very name conjures up majesty, beauty and wild abandon. That's certainly true of this part of the picturesque West Cork coast, between Skibbereen and Ballydehob. The Atlantic that washes in at the natural inlet here lives up to its name at times – roaring as mighty as a caged lion on stormy days.

In quieter moments though, the bay is calm and gentle, with the demeanour of a garden pond. Late in the year, after the seasonal winds and heavy rains of autumn have long passed away, and the crisp coldness of winter has set in, the afternoon sun peeks through the clouds, casting its golden glint over the waters. Its weakened rays highlight the misty outlines of the craggy mountains in the distance, painting their peaks with hazy purples and greens. The clear water in the heart of the bay, only about 20 feet deep in most places, is dotted with a flotilla of barrels. These are an indication of what goes on beneath the surface. Something rather delicious and wonderful grows in these unpolluted depths.

Colin Whooley is one of 13 mussel farmers whose crop forms the basis of a thriving shellfish industry in Roaring Water Bay. Colin grew up overlooking the bay, taking its charm for granted, and never even thinking about harnessing its natural elements to make a living for himself. It was only when he left school in 1990 that Colin, together with other like-minded men, explored the possibility of farming mussels in the backyard pond that nature had provided just a stone's throw from his family home.

'We all started small at first, putting ropes down to collect the natural spat fall of tiny mussels which was present here in the bay at certain times of year', says Colin. 'They clung to our ropes then we farmed them on from there. But the spat fall disappeared after a while, no one knows why, and now we each have to collect our baby mussels by hand every season.'

The uninitiated will wonder just exactly what that entails. Collection starts with finding the right location, usually an area of coastline where the ocean makes a big swell against rocks. That could be anywhere from the Mizen Head to County Kerry. Baby mussels, much smaller than a thumbnail, are brought back to Roaring Water Bay to be nurtured to adulthood. All 13 farmers run their own individual enterprises, though they often work together as a unit and help each other out as much as possible. 'We have a great working relationship with one another. If any of us needs a hand at any time, the others are only too willing to give it. We have grown up in this industry together, each learning from the other', says Colin.

Presuming that collection has been successful, Colin returns to the bay with his stock. The next stage involves pushing the tiny mussels into a fine-meshed stocking which is lowered into the bay and left for six months. During this time, the mussels grow big enough to be transferred to the mesh ropes which will be their home until harvest. These have much bigger holes and, as the mussels packed inside grow larger, they push their way through those holes, attaching themselves securely to the outside, each clinging on by its 'beard' or byssus.

It takes almost 18 months for a mussel to grow to maturity. During that time, the going can be tough and labour intensive, and even fraught with anxiety. In the height of winter, when the Atlantic is doing its very worst, the ropes, though anchored firmly to the sea bed, may be torn up in the unforgiving currents of this temperamental bay, and all the treasure of mussels attached are lost to the elements. Colin remembers the Christmas storm of 1997 as a particularly damaging one. While many West Cork residents were worried about when the power was coming back on and how they were going to cook the turkey, Colin was wondering how on earth the mussel farmers were going to pick up the pieces of their business that nature had chosen to scatter to the winds. 'Even though we've weathered storms down here, that one was bad. We all lost ropes, mussels and anchors that Christmas, but we helped each other out afterwards to try and secure what was left…'

Colin's mussel beds lie furthest away from the coast. At harvest, he must travel out on his fishing boat, specially adapted and equipped with all the tools that make gathering the mussels a much easier task than when he first started out. 'In the beginning, we did all the harvesting manually, heaving up the ropes to the surface one by one then scraping the mussels off them by hand. It was backbreaking', he remembers.

Nowadays, the hardest work is done by conveyor belt. Colin stands in a cabin attached to the back of the boat, lowered to the water's surface, then pulls the top of each rope up, attaching it to the belt. The belt's continuous

motion drags the entire rope, weighted down with mussels, along its corrugated length, removing the shellfish without damaging them. Many of the mussels in Roaring Water Bay are exported or go to supply shellfish factories which deal in the ready-cooked product. But Colin saves a proportion, the very cream of his crop to be sold fresh and live to the home market. He launched his company, Ocean Run, in 2005 and now his mussels have firmly established themselves as favourites with diners in the region's best restaurants, and fish lovers who shop in specialist fishmongers and supermarkets in the vicinity. Demand for the premium crop is high, and the quality even higher, due to the waters where the mussels are grown, and the handling they receive from Colin. The mussels

must be 'rehabilitated' after harvest, a process which requires patience whilst they adapt to being taken out of the water. Colin explains,

'When they first come out of the water on the ropes, all the mussels are open because they spend all their time feeding while constantly submerged. It takes them a while to learn how to close properly, and of course, if they can't close, they die. I keep them in crates on the shoreline for a few days after harvest. That way they get used to closing when the tide goes out, and opening to feed again when it comes in. It makes them stronger, and is absolutely essential if they are to be sold as a premium fresh live product.'

Colin checks the progress of the mussels regularly. Once he is absolutely satisfied that his mussels are ready for the next step, they come in to the small processing area just a 100 yards away from the shoreline. Here they are purified in a tank of salt water for 48 hours, another vital procedure required by law for any producer who specializes in fresh live mussels. These bivalves are notoriously prone to harbouring toxins present in sea water, and have been used in many countries as indicators and early warning signals of water pollution. All the mussels in Roaring Water Bay are tested regularly throughout their growth. At certain times of year, the waters around the coast of this country suffer from what locals call the 'Red Tide', a form of algae that washes in during the summer and can pollute for months. Its presence means closure of the bay and absolutely no harvesting until stock is once again clear of the toxins this natural phenomenon brings with it.

'So far we have been very lucky because for some reason, the algae washes in here then washes out again within a couple of days. It doesn't appear to like the environment. In some areas, it can stay for weeks, with devastating effects. We only usually have to close for about a week. But it's vital we test stocks constantly, all year round. This stuff is invisible to the naked eye, and doesn't harm the mussels, but would have serious consequences for humans.'

Roaring Water Bay, as a special area of conservation, is home to many different species of marine life, some of which come back to spawn here every season. The shallow, food-rich waters nurture baby haddock, cod, whiting and many other lesser-known fish species. Just off the shore lies a large and impressive area of rare coral, also protected by conservation laws. No wonder then, the waters of the bay are a natural draw for hobby divers and professional marine biologists alike.

A unique microclimate exists in the clear waters of this bay, undoubtedly a major contributing factor in making these fresh mussels taste as good as they do. Anyone lucky enough to buy a net of the tightly closed blue-black shelled delicacies need only steam them in a little white wine and garlic, for just a matter of moments, until the shells open to reveal the cooked, amber-coloured meats nestling snugly inside. All the accompaniment this seafood feast requires is plenty of fresh crusty bread to mop up the tasty juices after the last morsel has been nibbled from its shell. The mussels from Colin Whooley's ropes have all the flavour of the sea in which they were created. They are the epitome of delicious fresh local seafood, a sublime collaboration between the splendour of nature, and one man's commitment to harnessing and preserving it at its very best.

How to deal with Fresh Mussels

The preparation of fresh mussels is very often the thing that puts ordinary folk off buying them. There is no great mystery involved in handling them. It's not rocket science. And you certainly don't have to be a professional chef. If you never have a go at doing this, you are missing out on one of the best treats the sea has to offer.

The first and most important thing is to find good-quality mussels like Colin's that are absolutely fresh and tightly closed. You may spot one or two shells just slightly open. Give these a sharp tap – against the side of the sink or worktop – and it should have the effect of closing the mussel tightly. If it does not close, it means the mussel is dead. Throw it away immediately.

Cleaning mussels is simple. Assuming you have been through the 'sharp tap' routine and are happy that every mussel is now tightly closed, rinse the lot under cold, vigorously running water. Scrape off any dirt or other bits clinging to the shells with the back of a knife. Pull off the 'beard' which protrudes from each shell by tugging it sharply between thumb and forefinger. This 'beard' attaches the mussel to the rope as it grows.

Once the mussels are cleaned and 'de-bearded' they are ready to cook. For 1kg of mussels, to serve 4 as a starter or 2 as a main course, heat a splash of oil in a deep saucepan and gently fry 1 small peeled and chopped onion and 2 cloves of garlic until soft but not browned. Pour in half a glass of dry white wine. Bring to bubbling, add the mussels to the pan, cover with a lid and simmer for a few moments until all the shells open and the orange/gold mussel meats inside are clearly visible. Stir once or twice during cooking. After cooking, all the mussel shells should be open. If any have not opened, discard them. Do not try to prise them open. Season mussels with freshly ground black pepper and sprinkle with parsley. Serve immediately.

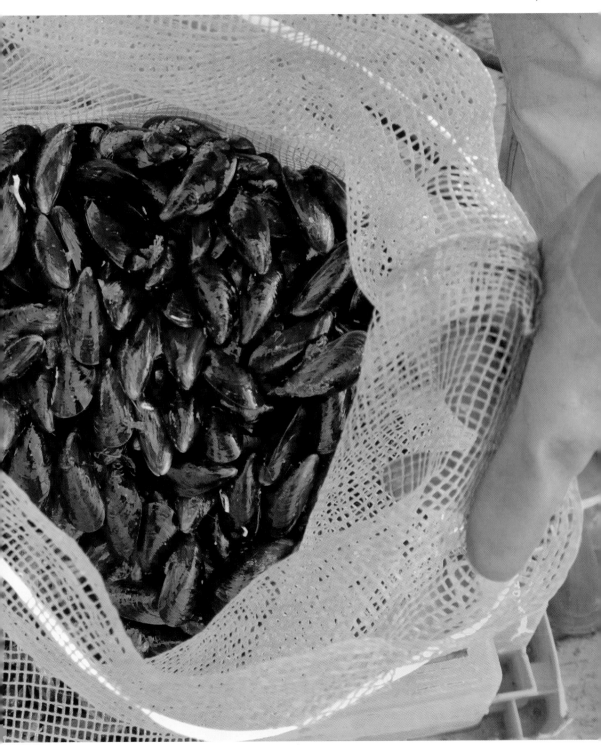

Fresh Mussels with Chilli and Coconut

This dish is prepared in exactly the same way as described but uses the Far Eastern flavourings of fresh chilli, Thai green curry paste and coconut milk to give a fabulous kick of spice. Serve it with some fragrant, boiled Jasmine rice, which you can stir into the bowls of spiced sauce after eating the mussels and slurp up from a spoon. Yummy!

Go through the preparation, cleaning and de-bearding routine. Once the mussels are ready to cook, set to one side. Heat oil in a deep saucepan and add onion, garlic and chilli. Cook gently until softened. Stir in Thai green curry paste. Cook for another minute. Add fish stock and bring to bubbling. Simmer for a few minutes. Add cleaned mussels, cover with a lid and simmer until all shells have opened. Stir once or twice during cooking. Pick out and discard any mussels that do not open. Stir in coconut milk and bring back to bubbling for a minute. Season and add lemon juice and coriander. Ladle mussels and their sauce into warmed bowls and serve with Jasmine rice.

SERVES 2

· 1 kg fresh tightly closed mussels
· 2 tbsp sunflower oil
· 1 onion, peeled and finely chopped
· 2 cloves garlic, peeled and crushed
· 1 small red chilli, seeded and finely chopped
· 1 tbsp Thai green curry paste
· 150ml/¼pt fish stock
· 150ml/¼pt coconut milk
· sea salt and freshly ground black pepper
· squeeze of lemon juice
· 1 tbsp coriander leaves, roughly torn

Seafood Rice

This is one of my very favourite ways of enjoying fresh fish and shellfish. Italian risotto rice is perfect for this because it absorbs all the fishy juices as it cooks. Look for arborio or carnaroli in delicatessens. In supermarkets, it's usually just labelled 'risotto' rice. The grains are much shorter and starchier, to give that yielding creaminess to the dish.

Clean mussels and make sure they are all tightly closed as described. Reserve.

Heat oil in a pan and fry onion and garlic until soft but not browned. Add rice and saffron and stir to coat in oily mix. Cook for a minute, then add wine. It should sizzle instantly. Bring to bubbling, then lower heat and simmer until wine is absorbed. Add a ladle of stock, then simmer this until absorbed. Continue like this until rice is almost tender, but not completely cooked through yet. Add cod, prawns and cleaned mussels, pushing them down into the rice. Cover with a lid and cook until mussels open, cod is opaque and prawns are piping hot, adding extra stock if necessary to finish cooking the rice until completely tender. Season and scatter over parsley to serve.

SERVES 4

· 450g/1lb live mussels
· 2 tbsp sunflower oil
· 1 onion, peeled and finely chopped
· 2 cloves garlic, peeled and crushed
· 350g/12oz risotto rice as above
· few threads of saffron
· 1 wine glass dry white wine
· 850ml/1½pt fish or chicken stock (approx.)
· 225g/8oz skinless cod fillet, in chunks
· 100g/4oz best large peeled prawns
· salt and freshly ground black pepper
· 1 tbsp finely chopped fresh parsley

Moules à la Crème

A classic way with mussels. The mussels give their juice to the white wine as they cook, then the whole lot is enriched with cream and flavoured with fresh parsley.

Prepare and clean the fresh mussels as described. Heat the butter in a pan and fry onion and garlic until soft but not browned. Add mussels and wine. Bring to bubbling, cover with a lid and simmer until mussels open fully. Stir in cream and parsley. Bring back to simmering, season with freshly ground black pepper, and salt if necessary, and serve immediately.

SERVES 4 AS A STARTER

· 1 kg fresh, tightly closed live mussels
· knob of butter
· 1 onion, peeled and finely chopped
· 2 cloves garlic, peeled and crushed
· 1 wine glass dry white wine
· 75ml/3floz cream
· 1 tbsp fresh finely chopped parsley
· sea salt and freshly ground black pepper

Spaghetti with Mussels and Tomatoes

The chilli in this simple, fast and gutsy supper is optional, but adds a racey taste to the sauce. I like it.

SERVES 4

· 1 kg fresh live mussels tightly closed
· 350g/12oz spaghetti
· 1 red onion, peeled and finely chopped
· 3 cloves garlic, peeled and crushed
· 1 small red chilli, seeded and finely chopped (optional)
· 3 tbsp good olive oil
· 400g can chopped tomatoes
· 1 tbsp tomato puree
· handful fresh basil leaves, torn, to finish

Clean and prepare mussels as described, making sure all are tightly closed. Cook pasta in lightly salted boiling water until just *al dente*. At the same time, in a large deep-sided saucepan, cook onion, garlic and chilli in olive oil until soft. Stir in chopped tomatoes and tomato puree. Bring to bubbling and simmer gently for a few minutes. Add mussels, cover and simmer until all are opened. Pick out and discard any that remain closed.

Drain pasta and drizzle with olive oil. Arrange in four warmed bowls. Spoon some mussels and juice over each one and scatter with torn basil.

More Ideas for Mussels

- You can use cooked shelled mussels for a salad with warm crispy bacon, rocket leaves and sherry vinegar dressing, as a lovely first course for four people. First make the dressing by shaking 1 tbsp sherry vinegar, 1 tsp Dijon mustard, 4 tbsp extra virgin olive oil and salt and freshly ground black pepper together in a screw top jar. Heap two good handfuls rocket leaves into a bowl. Clean 700g/1½lb mussels as explained, making sure they are tightly closed. Fry 6 roughly chopped rashers of streaky bacon crisp in 1 tbsp sunflower oil. While bacon is frying cook mussels in a splash of white wine in a covered pan until all are open fully. Pick out and discard any that remain closed. When bacon is ready, remove it from pan and drain on kitchen paper, keeping warm. Pick mussel meats from shells. Drizzle half the dressing over rocket and toss, then tumble onto four small plates. Divide mussels between plates, dotting over rocket, then drizzle with remaining dressing. Scatter over warm crispy bacon and decorate with whole flat parsley leaves.

- Top cooked mussels on the half shell with garlicky breadcrumbs and grill to brown. For four people, allow 8 mussels each as a first course. Clean, prepare and cook them in a covered pan with a good splash of dry white wine, until all shells open. Meanwhile, mix 175g/6oz fresh breadcrumbs with 4 cloves peeled and crushed garlic, 2 tbsp finely chopped fresh parsley, the grated zest of a lemon and freshly ground black pepper. When mussels are cooked, carefully remove one of the half shells from each, leaving meat nestling in the other half shell. Top shells with crumb mixture and drizzle with a little melted butter. Grill under a preheated grill until browned on top and serve immediately.

Special Delicacies

Special Delicacies

Only those who commit to producing the very best can be called true Creators. In the following pages, meet some of Ireland's original artisans – those who brought about change in the way her modern food culture has since been shaped.

Cheesemakers were among the first to start the revolution. Veronica Steele of Milleens forged the path for others to tread. Today, this country produces world class regional cheeses which make their gourmet mark far beyond the reaches of the island's boundaries. Each one is unique in its own taste and style, reflecting the personality of the area and the person who created it.

From those earliest days, we have seen a complete turn about in the way others perceive Ireland as a food nation. Now the country is known for gourmet produce to rival any continental destination. Yet another transformation has taken place on a much more basic front. Discerning food buyers have shown they welcome a return to the 'old fashioned' way in the fact that they have supported the emergence of the farmer's market movement nationwide. For many of today's consumers, a stroll round a local farmer's market to purchase from the stalls of home grown and produced goods is now as much a part of family shopping as the weekly trip to the supermarket. Yes of course there is still a place for supermarkets, and there will always be a need to use them. But surely it makes sense also to explore what an area has to give in terms of its regional foods, and to support those who created them? That is what living in a vibrant community is all about. Ask any Spanish, French or Italian housewife out shopping in her local market. She wants choice. She wants diversity. And so, it seems now, do we.

Thankfully, that diversity has at last come. We can enjoy all manner of home produced special delicacies, wherever in Ireland we happen to be, if only we bother to look for them. This section features some of the finest.

Anthony Creswell – Smoked Fish and Meat Producer

The village of Timoleague in West Cork shelters in the crook of the outlet of the Argideen River, where it meets the Atlantic Ocean. Its ruined medieval abbey, standing proudly on the shoreline, lends its Irish name of Tigh Molaige, 'House of Molaga' to the surrounding townland – so called because of its connection with Saint Molaga. The saint is reputed to have settled here and is credited with introducing the first bees to Ireland.

Just outside Timoleague village, *en route* to Bandon, Burrane, Inchybridge, is the home of Anthony Creswell, a second-generation artisan producer of superlative smoked fish and meats. Anthony's father Keith started the ball rolling in the 1970s, having relocated the family to West Cork from Essex, England, when Anthony was a teenager. Keith, who first came to Ireland to set up a chicken farming franchise nationwide, built chicken houses on his own land at Ummera, then experimented with smoking the meat of his home-reared birds in a small smoker he owned. Mr Creswell Senior was also a keen angler and began to cure and smoke the wild salmon he and his friends caught in Cork rivers, such as the Bandon, Blackwater and Argideen, which runs right by the family home. Keith spent time perfecting the smoking technique and, by the time the chicken franchise eventually folded, his smokery hobby had turned into a worthwhile business.

Anthony joined the family business some time later, after several years working in the wine industry in Europe and Australia, then setting up a wine company in Kinsale. Father and son spent almost 15 years working together establishing the Ummera range of artisan smoked produce and, as he says 'arguing all the time!' But it obviously did no harm – and, in fact, probably

contributed greatly to what is now an award-winning brand of Irish speciality foods recognized world-wide.

In 2000 Anthony relocated the smokery to a purpose-built timber frame unit just a few miles away from the Creswell family home at Ummera and an even shorter 'commute' from the house he shares with his wife Harriet and their young family. The house reflects Anthony's passion for the environment. Its eco-friendly timber frame structure faced with natural stone includes large areas of glazing in a passive solar design, and sits naturally into the landscape. His journey to work each day consists of a pleasant two-minute walk down the hill on a rough garden path, usually accompanied by the family's two Springer Spaniels, to reach the back door of the smokehouse. It certainly beats sitting in traffic on the motorway.

This tall, elegant Englishman strongly embraces environmentalism, incorporating 'green' practices at the smokery. Outside the smoke house, a vermi-composting unit, which uses worms to recycle all solid waste, is in operation. The unit is a simple and natural method of disposing of production waste, and the worms thrive on salmon trimmings, household scraps and a variety of other bits and pieces. To the front of the building, a natural wetland has been used to its best potential to deal with all waste water from the smokery. A series of small ponds with reeds, set into a woodland and wild flower area, filters waste water into clean water that can support wildlife and plants,

Ummera Smoked Product Range

Whole sides of smoked salmon, pre-sliced; smoked salmon slices in pre-weighed packs; smoked eel fillets, vacuum packed; crowns of smoked chicken, vacuum packed; smoked chicken drumsticks, vacuum packed; loin and streaky rashers of smoked bacon, vacuum packed; smoked back and streaky bacon joints, vacuum packed.

and provides a peaceful, natural setting in which to work. Anthony is also considering adding other eco-friendly elements to the premises in the future. His knowledge of what has now become a heart's desire was fuelled by his wife's interest in the subject. Whilst he jokes that former Trinity College Geography lecturer, turned Environmental Consultant, Harriet 'badgered him into it', you can't help but get the feeling that actually he's rather glad she did!

The environmental issue continues in Anthony's choice of products for smoking. Although he has produced smoked wild Irish salmon of superlative quality in the past, from now on he will concentrate on sourcing the finest organically produced fish. His fresh salmon comes from Clare Island, County Mayo where the fish are farmed organically, fed on natural feed and stocked in low density sea cages. It's a calculated decision based on his knowledge of declining numbers of wild stocks and, he feels, the way forward to attaining sustainable fishing for the area.

'If we continue to fish with driftnets out at sea when the wild salmon are returning to spawn we are reducing their chances of reaching their chosen river destination. When they are caught out at sea no one knows where they are heading, which makes it impossible to tell which rivers they are populating. My feeling is that we should not be fishing this way at all for the next number of years, in order to see if that has a positive effect of building up stocks. Fishing at the river estuary using draftnets can be better controlled. If we know a specific river needs a certain number of fish to maintain stocks, then any excess can safely be caught without damaging numbers. But we also need more fish counters in local rivers in order to keep these records.'

Continuing his father's tradition for smoked chicken, Anthony has recently re-developed this side of the business. He now smokes chicken breast 'crowns' and drumsticks, sourcing his chickens from a nearby supplier. The crowns, which consist of both breast fillets still attached to the bone, are first marinated in a fragrant and aromatic mix of organic Portuguese sea salt from the Algarve and Costa Rican organic cane sugar. Digging his hand deep into the barrel of fragrant, dark copper brown grains, Anthony explains how the sugar at first proved difficult to get into this country. It's now an essential component in the flavour of Ummera smoked chicken, adding a toffee caramel intensity to the meat. The sugar is used in the same recipe marinade for the drumsticks and organic salmon fillets, which must be processed completely separately and on different days from the other products, in order to maintain complete organic status. Anthony also smokes locally caught eel when stocks are available.

Timoleague's famous pork suppliers – Staunton's – provide the meat for Ummera smoked bacon. Noticing its dark brown colour, one can't help but wonder why it isn't the usual pale pink of other rashers. 'We don't use any nitrates or nitrites in production and that means the meat darkens during smoking. It's completely natural', Anthony explains. He first dry cures the bacon with sea salt, then smokes it for a long period at a low temperature over oak sawdust, to infuse a delicate taste. Even the sawdust is specially chosen for its lack of chemicals used in growing – and comes from wood grown in sustainable forests.

Anthony's views on the wild versus farmed salmon argument are ones he knows are not necessarily shared by fellow fish smokers, and says consumers will always make up their own minds which one they want to buy. If driftnet fishing of wild salmon ceases in the near future, he understands only too well that it will have a considerable knock-on effect on the livelihoods of commercial salmon fisherman, and those who rely on their catches. Ummera's special delicacies are created by a man who thinks logically and carefully about the impact his way of producing quality artisan foods may have on the planet. Many share his passion for conservation of wild fish stocks, agreeing that, clearly, this is a serious ecological issue that needs to be addressed soon. It's fair to say though that the debate will not be easy to resolve with a happy-ever-after ending. But Anthony Creswell has made definite decisions about the future of Ummera and the way he wants his business to progress. And, for that, he must be respected.

UMMERA
SMOKED
PRODUCTS

Smoked Chicken and Fresh Mango Salad

Refreshing lively flavours combine in this blissful summer salad. You may feel smoked chicken is an acquired taste – but, believe me, it won't take you long to acquire it. Always make sure your mangoes are perfectly ripe. They should have a little give in them when squeezed very gently in the palm of a hand. Mangoes can be awkward to stone. Hold the fruit down on a chopping board, steadying it firmly with the palm of an outstretched hand. With the other hand, take a sharp knife and run its blade horizontally against the flat of the large interior stone which you'll be able to feel reasonably easily. Remove the top slice of flesh, then turn the mango over and repeat on the underneath. You can cut off any flesh clinging to the ends of the stone then. You'll be amazed at how much of the total fruit is stone, but if the flesh is sweet and juicy, it's worth the trouble of getting at it!

Peel and stone the mangoes as described. Slice flesh thinly and place in a large bowl. Carefully remove the meat from the chicken crown and tear or slice the flesh into thin shreds. Add to the mango with rocket leaves, red onion and cucumber. Mix olive oil with vinegar, mustard, lemon zest and juice and herbs. Season with sea salt and freshly ground black pepper, and Tabasco sauce to taste. Spoon over salad and stir through gently to coat. Serve immediately with some crusty bread to accompany.

SERVES 4

- 2 large ripe mangoes
- 1 crown of smoked chicken
- 225g/8oz baby rocket leaves (the pepperier the better)
- 1 small red onion, peeled and finely chopped
- 5cm/2" piece fresh cucumber, finely diced

FOR THE DRESSING:
- 4 tbsp extra virgin olive oil
- 3 tbsp white wine vinegar
- 1 tsp Dijon mustard
- finely grated zest of half a lemon
- juice of half a lemon
- 1 tbsp finely chopped parsley or snipped fresh chives
- sea salt and freshly ground black pepper
- few drops Tabasco sauce
- chives for decoration

Smokey Chicken, Chorizo and Mussel Rice

The delicate smokey flavours here are absorbed into the rice and mussels with the white wine and tomatoes. This dish makes for scrumptious eating on a summer evening. Accompany it with a glass of elegantly crisp white wine from northern Spain. Delicious.

First prepare the mussels by removing the beards and cleaning under cold running water. Make sure they are all tightly shut. If any are slightly open, give them a sharp tap. Discard any that don't close. Reserve.

Heat oil in a pan and fry onion and garlic until soft but not browned. Remove from pan and reserve. Add chorizo pieces to pan and cook to brown. Stir in rice and cook for a minute or so to absorb the oil and flavourings. Pour over white wine, bring to bubbling and simmer gently until absorbed. Add tomato flesh and a ladle of the chicken stock. Bring to bubbling and simmer again until stock is absorbed. Continue adding stock gradually, simmering between additions until half is used up. Stir in the chicken and add prepared mussels. Add remaining stock gradually, cooking until rice is tender and mussels have opened. You may need a little more stock but be careful. You don't want rice that's too wet, just nicely moist, tender and coming together. Season with sea salt, freshly ground black pepper and a squeeze of lemon juice. Stir in parsley. Serve with salad and crusty bread.

SERVES 4

- 450g/1lb fresh mussels
- 2 tbsp sunflower oil
- 1 onion, peeled and finely chopped
- 2 cloves garlic, peeled and crushed
- 75g/3oz piece chorizo, in small chunks
- 275g/10oz short grain risotto rice (Italian arborio, Spanish Valencia)
- 1 glass dry white wine
- 3 ripe tomatoes, peeled, seeded and chopped
- 600ml/1pt chicken stock (approx.)
- 100g/4oz smoked chicken breast meat, removed from the bone and chopped
- sea salt and freshly ground black pepper
- squeeze of lemon juice
- 1 tbsp fresh parsley, finely chopped

Salmon Sushi

Elegant and ever-so-smart, these little bites make perfect nibbles with drinks before dinner. The preparation is a little fiddly, but the look at the end is amazing. The Japanese usually use thinly sliced raw salmon, but, if we're honest, our Western tastes haven't really embraced raw fish with the gusto of the Japanese! Smoked salmon works well instead. Sushi rice is usually found in delicatessens and specialist food shops.

Wash rice and cook according to pack instructions. It should be tender but still with bite. Drain well and place in a bowl. Mix dressing ingredients together and pour hot rice over, then stir through. Cool. When completely cold, separate grains with a fork, being careful not to break up the rice.

Lay a salmon slice out on a sheet of cling film, on a worktop. Spoon a little rice over, covering the slice but leaving a thin border at the sides and ends. Lay a few cucumber sticks in the centre of the rice, along the width of the salmon slice. Roll the salmon slice up tightly, using the cling film to enclose it. Prepare remaining salmon slices like this. Chill for a couple of hours. When ready to serve, remove cling film from rolls and trim ends neatly. Slice into small rounds and lay flat in a single layer on a plate, so you can see the rice and cucumber filling. Serve with pickled ginger and Japanese wasabi paste on the side.

You can vary the filling here by using cold scrambled egg to put in the middle instead of the cucumber sticks. Or do half and half for a change of flavours.

SERVES 4

· 175g/6oz sushi rice

FOR THE DRESSING:
· 3 tbsp Mirin (Japanese rice wine)
· 2 tsp sugar
· pinch of salt
· squeeze of lime juice
· 8 large slices of smoked salmon
· ½ cucumber, peeled and cut into thin sticks
· pickled ginger and wasabi paste for serving

Liver and Smokey Bacon

You either love liver, or loathe it. If, like me, you love it, then this dish, cooked with smokey bacon, onions, garlic and chopped tomatoes, is one of those comforting ones for a cold day. Use best quality lambs' liver. I always go by the colour, choosing liver that is pale-ish pinky brown rather than dark red/brown. Go to a good butcher to buy it and he'll usually slice off what you want from the whole liver. Always rinse and pat it dry when you remove it from the wrappings, and carefully cut out any tough tubey bits.

SERVES 4

· 2 tbsp sunflower oil
· 4 rashers smoked loin bacon, chopped
· 1 onion, peeled and finely chopped
· 2 cloves garlic, peeled and crushed
· 350g/12oz lambs' liver, thinly sliced
· seasoned flour for dipping
· 200g can chopped tomatoes
· 1 tbsp tomato puree
· 150mls/¼pt lamb or beef stock
· splash dry white wine
· sea salt and freshly ground black pepper
· 1 tbsp fresh finely chopped parsley

Heat oil in a large flameproof casserole and fry bacon until crisp. Remove and reserve. Add a little more oil to casserole and fry onion and garlic until soft. Remove this and reserve with bacon. Dip liver slices in flour and fry in casserole in batches, until browned and sealed. Return bacon and onions to casserole and pour over chopped tomatoes, tomato puree and stock. Add a splash of white wine. Bring to bubbling, then lower heat to simmer for 15 minutes, or until liver is tender. Season and stir in parsley. Serve with buttery mashed potatoes and broccoli.

CBLT

Premium smoked chicken and bacon, crunchy iceberg lettuce and ripest tomatoes come together in fresh crusty bread in this double decker, which elevates a lunchtime sandwich to new heights.

Pop bacon under a preheated grill until browned and crisp both sides. Meanwhile, cut 12 slices from the loaf and toast them until golden and crisp. Spread 8 with mayonnaise on one side only. Spread remainder with mayonnaise on both sides. Layer half the shredded lettuce and tomatoes over 4 base slices and pop the hot bacon on top. Sandwich with the middle slices of bread that have mayonnaise on both sides. Divide remaining lettuce and tomato between the four stacks, then arrange chicken on top. Top with final slices of bread, mayonnaise sides down and cut into triangles. Arrange on plates, points up, and serve immediately.

MAKES 4

· 8 rashers dry cure smoked back bacon
· a crusty loaf
· 4 tbsp mayonnaise
· ½ crisp iceberg lettuce, shredded
· 4 ripe tomatoes, sliced thinly
· 225g/8oz smoked chicken breast, in slices

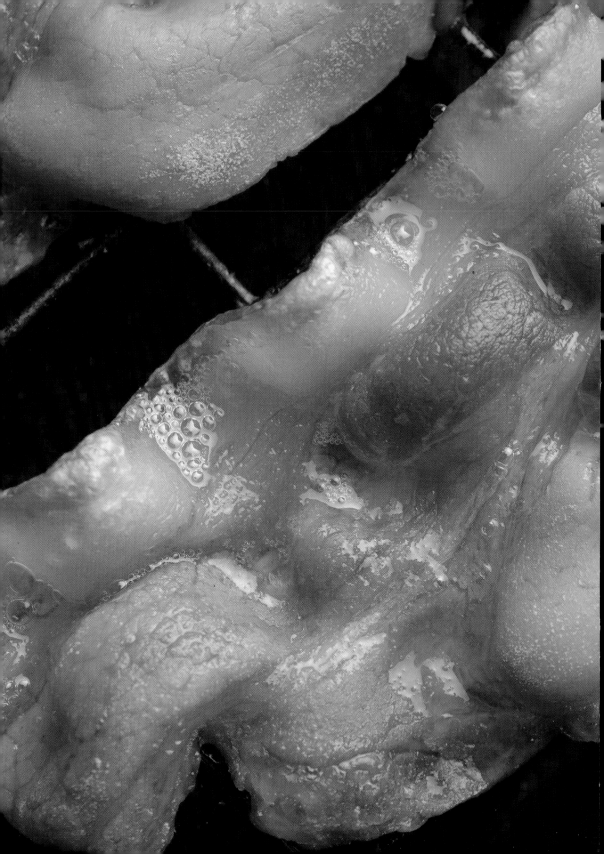

More Ideas for Smoked Chicken and Bacon

- Kids, in particular, seem to love smoked chicken drumsticks for their sweet, salty, smoky savouriness. I've found them a great addition to a school lunch box. My daughter came home from school rather disgruntled one day, having taken some for lunch, and politely requested that next time I gave them to her, could I make sure there was one for each of her classmates as well. They had all taken nibbles – and she'd ended up with no lunch. The proof of the pudding, hey?

- Smoked dry cure bacon adds a wonderful savoury flavour to meaty stews. For a stew for four, rind and finely chop a couple of back rashers and fry them crisp in hot oil in the bottom of the casserole. Remove the pieces and reserve, then use the flavoursome oil left in the base of the casserole, with a little extra splash of sunflower oil if necessary, to soften the onions and garlic, then brown the meat cubes before continuing on with the recipe, returning the bacon bits to cook in the stew.

- Remove the meat from a crown of smoked chicken breast and tear into shreds. Place in a bowl and toss with 2–3 tbsp mayonnaise, 1 tsp mild curry paste and 1 tbsp mango chutney. Season with freshly ground black pepper. Use as a delicious filling for fresh pitta breads, split and stuffed with plenty of crisp lettuce, cucumber and tomato slices first.

Tom, Giana and Fingal Ferguson – Cheese and Charcuterie Makers

West Cork is certainly the place to find the country's original artisan producers of cheese. Near the coast, where grazing pastures are moistened by sea mists and soft summer rains, the milk takes on a character all of its own. The flavours in the resulting cheeses echo the aromatics of wild herbs, the lush sweetness of clover and the freshness of that all-important Irish green grass.

Nowhere is this more evident than around the coastline of Schull. This countryside, rugged for the most part, affords a little grazing on fields going down to the water's edge. It's no coincidence that three of this country's most famous cheeses were created there at the very conception of the artisan food movement, and only a short distance – as the crow flies – from one another. Bill Hogan and Sean Ferry's Gabriel and Desmond are two of those cheeses. And Tom and Giana Ferguson's Gubbeen is the other.

Gubbeen House is a large farmhouse, the ancestral home of several generations of Ferguson family farmers. Tom Ferguson was brought up with farming in his blood, and loves nothing better than working on the land. His parents and grandparents were the same and offered employment and support to many a local family in need in the days when work in the country was scarce. Tom's wife Giana couldn't be more different, or so it would seem on the surface. Her childhood and early adulthood was spent between England and Spain – the first being the home she shared with her mother in London, the latter the country she travelled to regularly in order to visit her father. Looking back, she says Spain was where she learned to appreciate the complexity and diversity of local foods and experienced the pleasure of sharing meals around a large table with people who lived to eat. Though a formal upbringing in the heart of a European capital city might not seem to be the ideal stomping ground for a girl who grew up to become a 'hands on' farmer's wife, and one of Ireland's leading

pioneers of local and speciality foods, Giana has her mother's memories of living in the Staffordshire countryside and an inherent love of good home-made food to thank for the way life has turned out.

A formal Kensington education led to a promising career for Giana as an exhibition and event organizer with London's Institute of Contemporary Arts. The leap from trendy city living and working in the UK capital's prestigious art world to residing in a remote coastal region of Ireland was made quite by accident. 'My job was hectic and demanding, and I worked very hard at it because I absolutely loved it. But at one stage I decided to take a break from the heavy work schedule and came to West Cork to visit a friend in Ballydehob. That's when I met Tom.' That, indeed, was to prove a life-changing meeting and the two have been happily married for over 30 years.

Giana gave up London to move to Schull, and learned to adapt to life in the Irish countryside. Gubbeen cheese was born as a result of Giana and Tom's determination to diversify and increase the farm's productivity. The first cheeses, made with milk from Tom's own herd, were created in 1975 by Giana in her homely farmhouse kitchen. As production increased, a small outbuilding was converted as a cheese-making facility. The Dairy, as Giana fondly refers to the place where Gubbeen is now made, is located across the way from the kitchen. These days, its small entrance is adorned with an array of esteemed, circular plaques awarded over the years by Bridgestone Guide Irish food gurus, John and Sally McKenna. This small room bursts with life when cheese making is in full swing. The atmosphere has a happy buzz from energetic and enthusiastic people working at what they love doing. Behind the cheese-making area lies the curing room, where the finished Gubbeens are left to age for several weeks. Mature, ready-to-eat Gubbeen cheeses have a smooth, luxuriously creamy semi-sold style, and the microclimate in this particular part of West Cork adds to their rich and herbaceous flavour. The cheese rinds, formed during maturation, are known to support their own bacterial flora, identified recently and named as Corynebacterium Gubbeeni. These bacteria work their magic during ageing to create a diversity and individuality of taste in the cheese.

Alongside the original cheese, the farmhouse also produces a smoked version. Years back, local fish smoker Chris Jepson would smoke the cheeses on the Fergusons' behalf. When he decided to give up the business, he designed a smoker at Gubbeen, helped by Fingal. Giana continues the story, 'Fingal, who was young at the time, had often been down to watch the cheeses being smoked. He was always one of those inquisitive kids, forever asking questions! When we built the smoker at Gubbeen, Chris simply said "Don't worry, I'll make sure Fingal knows what to do." And he did!'

That early start led to a career in food production for the Fergusons' son, who now runs the famed and also much accoladed Gubbeen Smokehouse, a short stroll down the drive from the main house. The smokehouse is on the ground floor of Fingal's own home. Popular music playing loud over the preparation area is the first clue that this is the place of work of a young and vibrant team, headed by one of this country's new wave of second-generation food producers. And he takes his job very seriously. Before starting the smokehouse proper, Fingal spent time travelling abroad to learn his trade, adding to the experience he had already gained growing up. Now, in this specially built unit, where the smell of garlic and spices hangs in the air, he and his assistants create a fabulous range of continental salamis, chorizos, air dried hams, bacon and fresh sausages. At the end of the kitchen is the smoker and, alongside that, the specially equipped drying room, where the charcuterie hangs for several months. Windows are slatted with wooden blinds so as to let the fresh sea breeze in during the maturation process. The set-up is very similar to that in the north of Italy, where the famous salamis and air-dried hams are among the best in the world.

Outside Fingal's smokehouse, a box hedge-bordered herb garden, polytunnel and vegetable patch belong to sister Clovisse. Her home-grown organic herbs

Gubbeen Farmhouse Products

Gubbeen cheese, and Gubbeen smoked cheese, available in mild and mature versions. Fingal's Gubbeen Smokehouse products include dry cured smoked meats, salamis, hams, bacon and continental-style fresh sausages with various herb flavourings.

are used to flavour his charcuterie and she sells her organic vegetables at the local farmers' market during the height of the growing season. The Ferguson pigs provide tasty free range pork for Fingal's salamis and sausages. These happy creatures are kept in deep straw-bedded barns during the wettest months of winter, and let out to ramble in fields facing the Atlantic in summer. They are sociable animals that play with a football and love a rub on the back from any passing visitor. As well as their own special ration and tasty kitchen scraps, the pigs are treated regularly to the whey from the cheese making, just as in Parma, Italy. Its richness helps fatten and flavour the resulting meat.

In summer, the remaining pasture is dotted with Tom Ferguson's dairy cows, a mix of Fresian and rare, protected, Kerry Cows for which he has a real fondness. Giana's free range rare breed laying hens cluck contentedly in the yard and, coming up to Christmas, there will always be a handful of geese being reared for family and friends. This is a traditional and extremely productive farm, with, as Giana puts it, 'a bit of everything'. Every member of the family has a role. Rosie, another of the Ferguson girls, works on the administration side and keeps everyone organized. Giana says, 'It's wonderful that our children have come home to be involved in food production with us. We've always felt that this is an exhilarating way of life and we're delighted they seem to think so too. We're hoping to see the next generation of Fergusons on the land in future years.'

As well as finding time to be a wife, mother and creator of a world famous cheese, Giana was also a co-founder of the first Irish Slow Food Convivium, started in West Cork back in 1998, alongside Myrtle and Darina Allen. The role put her at the cutting edge of bringing local foods to the attention of Ireland – and, indeed, the world. She still takes an active part in all Slow Food events and is passionate about preserving local markets and protecting the rights of small producers. Most recently, she sat on the steering committee to devise University College Cork's Diploma in Speciality Food Production, first run in 2005, and the only one of its kind in Ireland to date.

For all those immense achievements, Giana is emphatic that her main job is as a farmer's wife, and she's quick to point out that the Ferguson farm was always a place of great resourcefulness in years long past. These days, it is so much more than that. There's a lot to be learned at Gubbeen House. At the heart of this innovative enterprise lies a farming family that loves to share its wealth of expertise, enthusiasm, and produce with those who live for truly great food.

Courgette, Gubbeen and Chorizo Frittata

Gubbeen's spicy chorizo and original farmhouse cheese combine for this frittata, the Italian version of Spanish tortilla, but thinner. I don't need to tell you to use fresh free range eggs, do I? You can pick up free range eggs in most supermarkets, and always in a farmer's market. Served cold, frittata makes a delicious portable feast for a picnic.

SERVES 4

· 1 tbsp olive oil
· 1 courgette, trimmed and, very thinly sliced
· 50g/2oz Gubbeen chorizo, chopped into small chunks
· 6 fresh free range eggs
· sea salt and freshly ground black pepper
· 50g/2oz Gubbeen cheese, rinded weight, grated

Heat oil in a non-stick frying pan and cook courgette gently to soften and brown lightly. Remove from the pan and reserve. Add chorizo, and cook to brown. Meanwhile, beat eggs with seasoning and add cheese. Pour off any excess fat from frying pan, leaving behind a tablespoon. Return courgette to pan and stir to mix with chorizo pieces. Pour in egg mix. Cook over medium heat until base is set and lifts from the pan when teased with a palette knife or fish slice. Place pan under a preheated grill, to cook the runny top until just set.

Remove pan from heat and cool slightly. Turn out by placing a large plate over pan, then inverting the pan so the frittata comes out easily. It will be upside down. Place another plate over the frittata, and turn the whole thing over so it's the right way up again. Serve in wedges, warm or cold.

Pasta Giana

When you have quality ingredients it's easy to create a fast supper that tastes like you're dining in a swish restaurant. This is one of those dishes, and couldn't be simpler, even for the most novice of cooks. It's named after Giana and uses Fingal's smokehouse fresh sausages finished with grated Gubbeen.

Cook sausages in a pan in the sunflower oil until browned all over and cooked through. Remove, cool slightly and slice. Cook pasta in lightly salted boiling water until just al dente. Meanwhile, make the sauce. Heat olive oil in a heavy bottomed saucepan and fry onion and garlic until soft but not browned. Pour over chopped tomatoes and wine. Bring to bubbling. Season, adding a pinch of sugar. Simmer until sauce is slightly reduced. Stir in the sausage slices and simmer for a couple more minutes to heat through thoroughly.

Drain pasta and transfer to a large serving bowl. Pour over the sausages and sauce and toss to coat and mix the pasta and sauce evenly. Scatter over parsley and sprinkle with grated cheese.

SERVES 4

· 4 Gubbeen Smokehouse fresh sausages
· 1 tbsp sunflower oil
· 350g/12oz penne pasta
· 2 tbsp olive oil
· 1 onion, peeled and finely chopped
· 2 cloves garlic, peeled and crushed
· 2 x 400g cans chopped tomatoes
· ½ wine glass red wine
· sea salt and freshly ground black pepper
· pinch of sugar
· 1 tbsp fresh finely chopped parsley
· 2 tbsp rinded and grated Gubbeen cheese

Smokehouse Pizzas

Don't let the making of the pizza dough put you off having a go at this. It's not difficult and simply requires planning rather than expertise. And I promise that when you've done it once, you'll never eat a bought pizza again. I've always said men make the best bread makers and only because they have the muscle required for kneading! It's not difficult though. Simply turn the prepared dough out onto a floured worktop. It will be flabby, misshapen and rough looking. Make it into a neatish mound, then start by stretching it away from you with the heel of your hand. Bring it back in towards you with a clenched fist, knuckles down. Avoid sticking your fingers into the dough as you knead, since this just makes it incredibly sticky. Keep going like this, turning it every so often. Once you get the hang of it, you'll know when your efforts are beginning to work because the dough will start 'fighting back'. This just means it begins to get springy and can better resist your attempts to stretch it. After ten minutes or so, it should be smooth and bouncy and ready to be left to prove. This takes a good hour plus, until risen and doubled in size, which is where the planning comes in. Most households, mine included, don't have the luxury of a proper stone pizza oven to make the pizza authentically crisp. But there is a cheat's way to achieve the desired effect. You need good quality baking sheets, which must be preheated in the oven first. The pizza bases can then be placed carefully on these, as explained below, and precooked for just a few minutes until they begin to firm up, before covering with the toppings. Nifty hey?

MAKES 4 LARGE PIZZAS

FOR THE DOUGH:
· 500g/1lb 2oz unbleached strong plain flour
· 2 tsp salt
· 1 sachet fast-acting dried yeast
· 2 tbsp extra virgin olive oil
· 2 tsp sugar
· 300ml/½pt warm water (not too hot)

FOR THE TOPPING:
· 300g/11oz jar ready-made organic tomato and basil sauce
· 100g/4oz thinly sliced Gubbeen salami or chorizo
· 1 red and 1 yellow pepper, seeded and thinly sliced
· 16 stuffed green olives
· 8 sundried tomatoes in oil, drained and cut into pieces
· few pickled Jalapeno chillies (optional)
· 300g/11oz smoked Gubbeen cheese, rinded and grated
· drizzles of olive oil
· dried oregano
· freshly ground black pepper

For the dough, sift flour into a bowl with salt. Add yeast and stir to mix. Stir olive oil and sugar into water. Gradually add to flour mix, bringing together to form a ball of dough. You might need a splash or two more of warm water to make all the flour stick together. Knead lightly to form a ball then turn out onto a floured worktop and knead for a good ten minutes as described. When it's ready, return dough to a clean bowl, cover with a tea towel and leave in a warm place until risen and doubled in size.

Punch the risen dough down by pushing a clenched fist into the centre. Knead lightly again for a few seconds to get a neat ball. Cut into four equal portions. Roll each out on a floured work top as thinly as possible. Preheat four large baking sheets in the oven, Gas 6/400°F/200°C. Sprinkle hot sheets with flour. Carefully transfer pizza bases onto their baking sheets by draping each one over a rolling pin, then laying it down flat. Bake for a few minutes until dough is beginning to crisp. Remove from the oven. Spread each pizza base with warmed tomato sauce then roughly scatter over some of each of the toppings. Sprinkle with cheese, drizzle with olive oil and sprinkle with oregano and freshly ground black pepper. Return to oven until bases are crisp and tops are golden and sizzling. Serve at once.

Fried Browns with Poached Eggs and Cheesey Tomatoes

This sauté potato dish is a delicious Sunday brunch idea – and a great way to use up leftover cooked potatoes. In fact, if you're having spuds with supper on Saturday evening, it's worth doing a few extra so they're ready for this treat on Sunday morning. If you've got new potatoes with the skins on, you don't have to peel them. When everything is ready, I like to put the soft fried eggs on top of the potatoes so when you cut into them, the runny yolks trickle over the pile. Yum.

SERVES 4

- 450g/1lb cooked waxy potatoes
- 2 tbsp olive oil, plus extra for drizzling
- 8 rashers dry cure smoked bacon, chopped into bits
- 1 tbsp finely chopped parsley
- sea salt and freshly ground black pepper
- 4 large ripe tomatoes, halved
- 4 tbsp grated smoked Gubbeen
- 4 fresh free range eggs
- extra chopped parsley to decorate

Cut potatoes into slices. Heat olive oil in a pan and fry bacon pieces until crisp and golden. Remove from pan and reserve. Add a little more oil to pan and cook potatoes over highish heat until golden brown, turning them during cooking. Return bacon and scatter in parsley. Season. Reserve, keeping hot.

Meanwhile, place tomato halves under the grill. Drizzle with extra olive oil and season. Cook until soft and lightly browned on top. Sprinkle with grated cheese and pop back under the grill to melt. Keep warm with the potatoes. Poach eggs soft in gently simmering water with a splash of vinegar added. Heap potatoes onto four warmed plates and perch an egg on top of each pile. Scatter with extra parsley and serve halved cheesey tomatoes on the side.

Fillet Steaks on Gubbeen and Chive Mash

Easy and heartwarming, these are good enough for a sassy Saturday night supper with friends. The beef should be local, and well hung to develop its true potential. Ireland is blessed with great butchers, some of whom even rear their own beef and also have their own slaughtering facilities. Try and locate one near you. All this dish needs is some wilted baby spinach leaves seasoned with sea salt, black pepper and a little grated nutmeg to add subtle, warm spiciness.

Steam potatoes over a pan of boiling water until very tender. Transfer to a bowl and mash with milk and butter. Stir in cheese and chives. Season and cover the bowl, keeping potatoes hot.

Heat oil in a heavy bottomed pan and cook steaks over high heat to sear and brown on both sides. For medium steaks, cook until pricks of blood appear on the cut surface of the meat. The texture should be 'giving' but not flabbily soft, when the steak is prodded with a finger. Season with sea salt and freshly ground black pepper. Spoon little mounds of mashed potato on warmed plates, top with fillet steaks, and pour pan juices around. Serve with baby spinach leaves wilted in a knob of butter in a hot wok, and seasoned with sea salt, freshly ground black pepper and freshly grated nutmeg.

SERVES 4

- 700g/1½lb potatoes, peeled weight, in chunks
- splash of fresh milk
- good knob of butter
- 50g/2oz grated Gubbeen cheese
- 1 tbsp fresh snipped chives
- sea salt and freshly ground black pepper
- 2 tbsp sunflower oil
- 4 fillet steaks

More Ideas for Gubbeen Products

- Enjoy a continental-style lunch of Gubbeen cured meats and cheese out in the garden on a sunny day. Choose from the selection of air dried ham, cured pork loin, chorizo and salami, arranging thin slices on a large plate. Add a few slices of Gubbeen cheese, smoked or plain, whichever you prefer. Garnish the meats and cheese with tiny white cocktail onions and whole caperberries, served in a little dish on the side. You need plenty of crusty bread and a little dish of extra virgin olive oil seasoned with sea salt and cracked black peppercorns for dipping as you eat.

- Like all cheeses, it's best to leave Gubbeen out of the fridge for a good half hour before you want to serve it on a cheese board. It needs that time to come to room temperature and give of its best in the taste department. Accompany both the smoked and plain versions with crunchy apple wedges or sprigs of red grapes. A few Brazil or hazelnuts are good too.

Bill Hogan and
Sean Ferry – Cheesemakers

The land around the coastline of Schull has a generous nature, washed by warm currents, which create a distinctive microclimate. It's not unusual on Christmas Day to take a walk on the beach with temperatures in the low 60s. The mild weather has supported the region's farming community for many generations, long before Schull village became an internationally famous holiday destination, or the permanent home of the many celebrities and non-nationals who now make up the local community. The original inhabitants were born and bred and possessed a certain self-reliance that allowed them to thrive and trade across the water from earliest times.

Artisan cheesemaker Bill Hogan, a native New Yorker whose Irish roots go way back, has lived in the Schull area for almost 20 years, and possesses that same self-reliance in spades. He and his cheese-making partner Sean Ferry are vanguards of the Irish artisan food movement, producing the famous Gabriel and Desmond cheeses in this region since the late 1980s. But in the last number of years, life and cheese making has been far from straightforward for these two creators, who are at the top of their profession in speciality food production.

Bill and Sean studied their art on the High Alp in Switzerland in the summer of 1987, with their Swiss Cheesemaster Josef Enz. Bill had trained previously under Josef Dubach, receiving an invitation to learn how to make cheese under the guidance of this internationally respected Cheesemaster, in exchange for translating his book on traditional cheese production in the Andes into English. After a period of intense training, the two returned to Ireland to make cheese, first in Donegal. Bill began to research the possibility of coming to West Cork,

knowing the milder climate and quality of milk was perfect for the type of cheese he and Sean wanted to make. They had already had some success with their Donegal cheeses finding a market with discerning foodies in Dublin, though milk was becoming increasingly difficult to source.

The move eventually came at a time when farmhouse cheese production in the area was in revival. A successful property search hunt unearthed a gem of a farmhouse that Bill says they both knew instantly would be 'perfect for cheese making'. Situated a short distance from the ocean, and sheltered to the front by wild fuchsia and honeysuckle hedges, the two chose the building for its practicality, recognizing at once its potential to accommodate special cheese-making equipment to be installed in the converted ground floor rooms. But the deciding factor was the original stone carriage house next door, dating back to 1900, and immediately earmarked to become the curing room for maturing cheeses. Today it stands proud in the courtyard, its aged, weather-beaten walls swathed in a grapevine hanging heavy with bunches of Muller Thurgau grapes ripening in the sun.

Summer milk came from farmers in the immediate locality, whose cows grazed on grass, wild flowers and herbs so typical of this terrain. The grazing was akin to that of the Alpine dairy herds whose milk created cheeses the pair had learned about in Switzerland. Only specially selected unpasteurized summer milk goes into Gabriel and Desmond, and this was delivered to the farmhouse dairy early each morning. These exclusive cheeses became known for their complexity and length of flavour, and soon rose to fame. Chefs wanted Gabriel and Desmond on their menus, discovering that in cooking they lost none of their character and, in fact, had penetrating, long-lasting tastes that did not diminish. Specialist delis here and abroad cried out to stock them, with Manning's Emporium in Ballylicky being one of the first West Cork shops to introduce the cheeses to the locality. Cheese connoisseurs, such as Randolph Hodgson of Neal's Yard London, Monica Murphy, owner of one of Dublin's first specialist cheese shops, Damien Carroll

A Taste Of Two Great Cheeses

Gabriel
Named after Mount Gabriel, this extra hard cheese has complexity of flavour and gentle spiciness, with a lasting aftertaste perfect for cheese sauces and fondue. Bill and Sean recommend an equally spicy white wine made from Alsace's unique Gerwurztraminer grape, or a Pinot Gris or Riesling to complement the taste of Gabriel.

Desmond
This cheese makes a bold statement on the tongue, full of piquant pepperiness and mouthfilling richness and heat. Try it shaved thinly over a salad of baby rocket leaves dressed simply with best olive oil and balsamic vinegar, sea salt and freshly ground black pepper. Or serve just as it comes, with a glass of European red wine or, again, an Alsatian white wine.

of Superquinn and Eugene Carr of Traditional Cheese distributors, were already big fans. Over the years, the popularity of the cheeses went from strength to strength, receiving reviews from Irish food writer Theodora Fitzgibbon, and Henrientta Green, pioneer of small producers in the UK and author of the *Food Lovers' Guides to Britain*, among others. Then, five years ago, events occurred which were to severely threaten the survival of these great cheeses almost irreversibly…until Bill Hogan's self-reliance and dogged resilience leapt to the fore.

In 2002 an outbreak of Bovine TB hit the Schull area. On various occasions, local herds came down with positive tests. Each time this happened, the Department of Agriculture retroactively detained Bill and Sean's cheeses going back to the last clear test, which, in some cases, affected cheeses going back over a year. As a result, almost all the cheese in the ancient curing room could not be sold. On examining the law and reading the small print of the orders, the two men found they had the right of appeal. The science of the production of the cheeses showed emphatically that TB could not survive the thermophilic process by which they are made. A long and costly legal battle ensued, during which time the men appealed five detention orders and one prohibition order. Three Irish judges were involved in hearing their evidence, together with that from high-profile scientists brought in to present the facts as they stood. During this difficult time, the cheesemakers had unanimous support from the country's food writers, chefs, and of course, all their regular customers, for which they remain extremely grateful. The cases were hard fought – and winning meant devoting every possible spare moment to the cause. This, in itself, put pressure on cheese production. But finally, after two years of court appearances, including hearings of appeals made by the Department of Agriculture, Judge Terrence Finn of Clonakilty District Court declared the cheeses were, in fact, fit for consumption. It was an enormous result, and the case has now set a precedent for small producers, who often suffer in what Bill calls 'a climate of persecution'.

Since 2005, production has transferred to Newmarket Co-Op in north-west Cork. The two men were invited by the Co-Op to move their operation to the area, well known for its superlative grassland, and avail themselves of the finest quality milk for their cheeses. Bill and Sean moved lock, stock and copper vat to the new home of Gabriel and Desmond, and both are delighted with outcome and location. 'At Newmarket we have our own special room with traditional copper vats and presses and we only use specially selected unpastuerized summer milk from this area, which is some of the best in Ireland.'

Gabriel and Desmond cheeses are thermophilic, produced by first introducing a special starter culture and vegetarian rennet to the milk. The mix must then be left to rest, and Sean intervenes at this point, pushing a paddle into the swirling mass to settle its movement and allow the curds to form. Curds are cut, stirred, then slowly heated to a high scald. The right amount of heat plays a huge role in the individuality of flavour in each cheese. Desmond is finished at a lower temperature. Experience and a certain, natural 'feel' for the task is necessary to recognize exactly when the curds are ready to be hooped from the whey. This is done by hand, using a sheer muslin cloth to lift them in a steaming mass and allow for draining before the next stage begins. Drained curds are packed carefully into large moulds then hand pressed with a giant, wall-mounted alpine screw press, into the familiar huge wheels so typical of this type of cheese. In the temperature-controlled curing room, fresh cheeses are transferred to a brine solution for anything up to three days, depending on size, to allow the hard outer rinds to form, then moved to specially made slatted wooden shelves for the first part of their maturation. After a few months, cheeses are returned

to the curing room in Schull, where they remain for anything from ten months to three years.

The curing room holds a treasure trove of magnificent cheeses at varying degrees of ripeness, reclining until exactly the right moment of readiness. Some weigh 35–40 kg, with little ones between 5 and 15 kg. Each is marked with the year of production. As Bill strolls through, he gives each a loving stroke, a gentle, fatherly tap and knows intuitively when each will be at its peak. In cheese making, this practice, Bill explains, 'says a lot about how the cheese is proceeding from the way it resonates.' Bigger cheeses take so much longer to reach full ripeness, but the resulting flavour is better and bolder. 'They seem to have a more developed, fudgier taste', he says. 'We now know thermophilic cheeses like these were made in Ireland up to the famine, when the art was lost.' Thanks to the determined attitudes and pioneering efforts of Hogan and Ferry, the practice has been revived and future production now seems certain. Long may it continue.

West Cork Cheese Fondue

Fondue has made a recent comeback after years in exile. Its reputation as the snooty, aspirational dish served at parties thrown by bored housewives who wanted to impress the neighbours has thankfully long since passed away. Now this dish of melted cheese is at the hub of the most sociable, relaxed gatherings, best enjoyed with a handful of close friends who don't mind getting the dribbles down their chins! Gabriel or Desmond cheeses, or a mix of both, work well in this recipe.

Rub fondue pot with cut sides of garlic. Add wine and heat gently to almost bubbling. Turn down heat. Gradually add cheese, with cornflower, stirring to melt. Continue like this until all cheese is added, stirring until smooth. Add Kirsch and season with freshly ground black pepper. Serve in the pot with a heap of crusty bread cubes, steamed asparagus tips, broccoli and cauliflower florets and sautéed mushrooms for each guest to dip in on the end of a fork. Get everyone to take a turn stirring the fondue while eating.

SERVES 4–6

· 1 clove garlic, peeled and halved
· 300ml/½pt dry white wine
· 450g/1lb rinded weight of Desmond or Gabriel cheese, or half and half, grated
· 1 tbsp cornflower
· 1–2 tbsp Kirsch (optional)
· freshly ground black pepper
· cubes of crusty bread, steamed asparagus tips, broccoli and cauliflower florets and sautéed whole button mushrooms to serve

Rocket and Peach Salad with Gabriel Cheese and Honey Vinaigrette

Baby rocket is essential for this simple summer first course salad. Its pepperiness and piquancy can't be beaten, offsetting the juiciness of the peaches perfectly. Spanish peaches, in season, are worth seeking out. Otherwise choose fragrant Italian peaches, just at the point of ripeness. Long-matured Gabriel cheese shaves just like parmesan and lends a hint of salty nuttiness to the finished salad.

Halve the peaches and remove the stones. Cut each half into thin slices. Place in a bowl with rocket and spring onions. Mix the vinaigrette ingredients in a screw top jar, shaking vigorously. When you are ready to eat it, dress the salad with the vinaigrette and toss lightly with finger tips. Heap onto a platter or into a salad bowl and shave over the Gabriel cheese. Eat at once.

SERVES 4

- 3 ripe peaches
- 225g/8oz baby rocket leaves, rinsed and spin dried
- 6 spring onions, trimmed and sliced thinly on the diagonal
- small piece Gabriel cheese

FOR THE DRESSING:
- 1 tsp runny honey
- ½ tsp wholegrain mustard
- 1 tbsp white wine vinegar
- 4–5 tbsp extra virgin olive oil
- sea salt and freshly ground black pepper

Chive Omelette with Bacon and Gabriel Cheese

Bliss of blisses. This is an easy Sunday morning breakfast, or would definitely do nicely as a light supper with crusty bread and a salad. Choose free range eggs and best quality dry cure bacon, preferably free range, if possible.

Grill bacon rashers crisp. Reserve, keeping hot. Beat eggs with milk, seasoning and chives. Melt butter in an omelette pan and add egg mix. Stir mixture with a fork from edge of pan to the middle until base sets and top is still slightly runny in the centre. Scatter Gabriel cheese over one half and top with crispy rashers. Flip over other half of omelette and cook for another minute to lightly melt the cheese. Shake the pan gently to prevent the omelette sticking. Slide out onto a plate and serve immediately.

MAKES AN OMELETTE FOR ONE

· 2–3 dry cure back bacon rashers
· 2 large free range eggs
· splash of milk
· sea salt and freshly ground black pepper
· 1 tbsp fresh snipped chives
· knob of butter
· 2 tbsp grated Gabriel cheese

Golden Roasted Roots

This is a wintry combination of parsnip, carrot and potato, roasted golden and given a generous sprinkling of grated Desmond towards the end of cooking time, then returned to the oven to melt and add delicious, savoury crunch. You can peel the potatoes if you prefer, but I think they are more rustic not peeled. Serve these veggies with good roast beef, preferably a well-hung rib on the bone, for a majestic special occasion meal.

Halve parsnips and carrots lengthways then cut into quarters to make fat 'chips'. You might need to cut the parsnips into eighths if they are very big. Place in a bowl with garlic cloves and onion wedges. Drizzle with olive oil and season. Toss and reserve. Cut potatoes into big chunks and parboil these for a few minutes in lightly salted boiling water. Drain and shake in a colander to rough up the edges. Drizzle with olive oil and season. Strew all veggies in a large roasting tray. You might need two. Place in a preheated oven, Gas 5/375°F/190°C for 25 minutes or almost tender. Scatter in Desmond and return to oven until completely tender. Transfer to a serving dish and sprinkle over extra grated Desmond and some fresh thyme leaves.

SERVES 4

- 2 parsnips, peeled
- 3 carrots, peeled
- 8 whole fat cloves garlic
- 1 onion, peeled and in wedges
- 3–4 tbsp olive oil
- sea salt and freshly ground black pepper
- 2 largish potatoes, scrubbed
- 75g/3oz rinded weight of Desmond cheese, grated, plus extra to finish
- 1 tbsp fresh thyme leaves

Mushroom and Parma Ham Risotto with Desmond Cheese

Big field mushrooms were invented for this comfort dish of all comfort dishes, in my book anyway. Don't be frightened of making risottos. They have the reputation of being difficult, but they aren't if you have the right rice. Buy arborio or carnaroli, which come from Italy and are available in some supermarkets, and good delis. These two are starchy short grain rices, essential for that characteristic creaminess in the finished dish. Many cooks would say a perfect risotto should be almost soup-like in consistency. But it's a personal choice. My idea of brilliance is the 'in-between' stage – enough soft runniness for it to be a pleasure to eat – without having to slurp it up on a spoon.

Heat oil and butter in a pan and fry onion and garlic until soft but not browned. Add mushrooms and cook to soften. Add rice, stirring to mix in the grains. Gradually add a ladle of stock. Bring to bubbling, then simmer until absorbed. Repeat with more stock, bubbling to absorb. Continue like this until all absorbed and rice is tender. Keep an eye – it may need more or less stock. Add parma ham strips, basil leaves, butter and cheese. Season with salt and freshly ground black pepper. Serve with extra grated Desmond cheese for topping.

SERVES 4

- · 1 tbsp oil
- · good knob butter
- · 1 onion, peeled and finely chopped
- · 2 cloves garlic, peeled and crushed
- · 225g/8oz field mushrooms wiped and sliced
- · 225g/8oz arborio rice (risotto rice)
- · 850ml/1½pt vegetable stock (approx.)
- · 4 wafer thin slices parma ham, cut into strips
- · fresh basil leaves
- · extra knob of butter
- · 50g/2oz grated Desmond cheese, plus extra for serving
- · sea salt and freshly ground black pepper

Fish Pie with Cheesey Mash

Always buy fish from a reputable fishmonger who knows where and when it was caught and can skin and fillet expertly. It doesn't matter which of Bill and Sean's cheese you use for this. Choose your favourite.

Season potatoes with salt and steam until tender. For the sauce, melt butter in a pan and add flour. Cook for a minute then gradually add milk, stirring to thicken. Add dill, cream and seasoning. Meanwhile, poach the fish in the white wine and water in a covered pan over gentle heat until cooked through. Lift out fish with slotted spoon and fold carefully into sauce with prawns and quails' eggs. Spoon into an ovenproof dish.

When potatoes are cooked, mash with butter, egg yolk, and milk until smooth. Add cheese and seasoning. Spoon over fish and sauce, fluffing top with a fork. Sprinkle over extra cheese then bake in a preheated oven, Gas 5/375°F/190°C for 20 minutes or until top is golden and filling is piping hot.

SERVES 4

FOR THE TOP:
· 900g/2lb floury potatoes, peeled weight, in chunks
· sea salt and freshly ground black pepper
· generous knob of butter
· 1 egg yolk
· splash of milk
· 50g/2oz grated Gabriel or Desmond cheese, plus a little extra

FOR THE FILLING:
· 350g/12oz skinless cod or haddock fillet, in chunks
· 350g/12oz fresh skinless salmon fillet, in chunks
· 150ml/¼pt dry white wine and water mixed
· 100g/4oz best peeled prawns
· 4 hard boiled quails' eggs, peeled and halved

FOR THE SAUCE:
· 40g/1½oz butter
· 40g/1½oz flour
· 425ml/¾pt milk
· 1 tbsp fresh dill, chopped
· 4 tbsp cream

More Ideas for
Gabriel and Desmond Cheese

- These cheeses work very well on pasta dishes, just like parmesan. Grate the cheese finely then place in a bowl on the table so everyone can help themselves to what they want.

- Caesar Salad is a classic which usually uses parmesan. But the hardness of Gabriel works just as well.

- Use a vegetable peeler to make long shavings of Gabriel or Desmond to pop into salads. They look very glamorous shaved onto a plate of thinly sliced tomatoes with a few sliced green olives thrown over as well, before dressing with olive oil, red wine vinegar, sea salt and freshly ground black pepper.

Declan Ryan – Artisan Baker

The streets of Montenotte perch high over Cork. Any residence here has a bird's-eye view of the river, its traffic and the buzzing city beyond. In this prime location, one house stands out from the rest, though not simply for its undeniable 'des-res' status. Its discreet frontage gives no clue. Just alongside it, down the steep flight of old stone steps, beyond the private garden and through an ancient wrought iron gate, an unassuming, lock-up 'garage' forms the next piece of the puzzle. But even this small building doesn't give the secret away. Today its large double doors are firmly secured, its innards silent and empty. A light dusting of flour on the tiled floor might just hint at what went before. This tiny space was the birthplace of the best bread in Ireland today.

How could we live without bread? When we're feeling peckish, there's something fundamentally nurturing about crunching into a slice of thick toasted crusty, still hot, and with a slathering of butter deep enough to melt in pools on its surface. At lunchtime, the quickest way to quell the pangs is to sandwich a couple of slices together with a few slivers of extra mature cheese or some best butcher's ham in between. Those with the taste for it might even just tear off a hunk and eat it as it comes, or with a drizzling of richly green, peppery, single estate extra virgin olive oil. Whatever your penchant for bread, one thing is certain. We all rely on it every single day.

A pity then, that most of what's available is usually mass produced, cotton-wool textured and deserves no accolades. In fact, speaking at a past seminar, Derek O'Brien, Head of the National School of Baking at DIT, reportedly said

that over 80 per cent of what was now produced for public consumption he refused to call bread. The success of 'in-store bakeries' shows just how much we crave the real thing, freshly baked and preferably still warm when we buy it. But are we so deprived as to be happy to make do with a pseudo-French version – supplied to the shop in dough form and needing only the effort of a pair of hands to pop it in the oven? It would seem so. Too bad we're so easily pleased.

Take the French themselves, and their European cousins Spain and Italy, for that matter. It's normal to find at least one bread shop, and not unusual to discover several, in any one town or village in any of these countries, where loaves are made on the premises, from scratch, every day. Sometimes, even twice daily, when the traditional afternoon siesta is observed in the heat of summer. If they can do it, why can't we? Where have all our bakers gone?

Declan Ryan is Ireland's saving grace. He has breathed the kiss of life into the dead art of real bread making in this country. He is Cork's own Master Baker. And a maestro he is. Many will recognize the Arbutus name from Cork city's prestigious, Michelin-starred Arbutus Lodge restaurant in Montenotte, where Declan was owner/head chef until his retirement in 1999. Trawl through his CV from before then, and it reads like the *Who's Who?* of fine eating establishments. Starting out at the Russell Hotel, London, Declan then went on to become Stagaire at the hotel of the same name in Stephen's Green, Dublin. A spot of restaurant hopping followed, with stints at the Avis Hotel Restaurant in Lisbon,

Brittania Hotel, London and, finally, the oh-so-smart Les Frères Troisgros in Roanne, France. So you see, when retirement finally came, this man was never going to take it lying down. With the business sold and time on his hands, he needed a hobby, 'Just to keep the brain ticking over', he smiles.

Having been inspired as a young lad by his West Cork granny from Dunmanway, who baked brown soda bread whenever he visited, Declan fancied his chances in the bread-making department. 'She made the most wonderful bread, to a simple recipe. I can also remember my Grandfather taking wheat they had grown to the mill in Macroom to be ground'. These memories and the urge to get his hands dirty in the kitchen again were to form the beginnings of his new pastime.

The Arbutus Bread Gallery

San Francisco sourdough loaves, in rounds, or large rings with holes in the centre; organic spelt bread (suitable for wheat-intolerant diets); rye bread; Pain Tradition; tomato bread; Granny Ryan's West Cork Brown Soda Bread.

Super Sarnies

Good bread like Arbutus needs no adornment – but it really is the business when it comes to first-class sandwiches. If you live in the Cork area, check the directory at the back for stockists. For those outside the county, hunt down the best local baker you can find. Your nearest farmer's market is a good place to start!

Declan's one time two-car lock-up garage, beside the imposing family home in Montenotte, was specially converted to form a small bakery. At first, he delivered the freshly baked, still warm loaves himself in a jeep to a customer base totaling less than a handful of clients. What he didn't count on was phenomenal success. Declan Ryan refuses to bow to fakery in bakery. That's why his post-retirement hobby has become a full time, award-winning business.

Using only the finest, unbleached flours and time-honoured methods, Declan produces for the best delis and restaurants in Cork. Working alongside Head Baker, Pavel Patrouski, who baked previously in San Francisco, and artisan bakers Ivors Tirums, Sukru Takak and his own son Darragh Ryan, Declan churns out at least 800 loaves a day, often nearer to 1000 on the weekends. The chefs at Isaac's, Clancy's and Boqueria in Cork are all big fans. It's not difficult to see why. Every loaf is proved naturally, shaped by hand and baked to crusty perfection the old-fashioned way. His famous sourdough, crusty French baguettes, fragrant tomato breads, wholesome rye and spelt breads and, of course, that good old Irish brown soda, have not so much as a hint of the chemical additives or improvers much relied upon by other, corner-cutting bakers.

You can find the Arbutus bakery by the unmistakable, lactic smell of the culture Declan uses to make his San Francisco sourdough rise. It's a special ferment called an 'autolyse', created from organic grapes, flour and water. 'I started the one we use over ten years ago, and top it up every day', Declan explains. Arbutus sourdough is many long hours in the making, the mass of the dough resting for at least four hours before the final mixing and hand shaping into individual loaves. Each one, placed in a cloth-lined basket, proves slowly overnight in the fridge at a low temperature, gradually warming up a few degrees for the last few hours before baking. 'Sourdough is hearth baked straight on the hot stone, creating an instant rise in temperature as soon as the bread hits the oven, to achieve the right texture and crust' he says. Removal from the oven is done with a traditional wooden 'peel' – a long-handled implement with a circular, paddle-shaped end, which can reach right to the back of the oven to retrieve each round golden loaf as soon as it's ready. His Pain Tradition, which uses a percentage of sourdough, is shaped into typical, long French sticks with diagonally slashed tops, their bases dusted in crushed olive stones before baking. This technique was learned from Declan's friend and fellow bread maker in the French village where he and his wife also have a home. His inspirational granny is forever immortalized with 'Granny Ryan's West Cork Soda Bread', a traditional soda and buttermilk brown loaf made to her very recipe.

The runaway success of Arbutus Breads has forced Declan's decision this year to vacate the long outgrown original bakery for larger premises nearby. His aim is to increase supply to meet demand for his unique handmade product, without compromising the high quality already established. 'We are now a truly state-of-the-art bakery and the new equipment has taken away much of the time-consuming back-break work we had before. That enables us to be more productive in creating highest standard artisan breads from natural products sourced locally, as they always have been.'

This man's baking expertise is so well respected that, in 2003, he was appointed to the Academic Council of the Dublin School of Baking. He's also a member of the Artisans Committee of the Food Safety Authority of Ireland, an associate member of the Richaume Club of Ireland Craft Bakers and an active member of the Bread Bakers Guild of America.

Declan Ryan is the bread lover's God. His bread, once tasted, is not so quickly forgotten. Those other 'freshly baked' imitations – no matter how hot from the oven they may be – pale beside it. Bite into a hunk of Arbutus San Francisco sourdough to accompany a warming broth. Break off a chunk of real Pain Tradition and enjoy it with charcuterie or a little just ripe brie, soft-rinded, creamy and oozy in the middle. Spread a bit of salty Irish butter on Granny Ryan's Brown Soda. Bring on Heaven.

San Francisco Sourdough Steak Sandwich

Meaty, macho, and oh so hunky, this takes some beating. If smooth mustard doesn't cut it for you, try some crunchy wholegrain instead.

MAKES 1

· ½ small onion, peeled and thinly sliced
· sunflower oil
· 2 thickish slices Arbutus sourdough
· Dijon mustard
· a mix of lettuce leaves (lollo rosso, oakleaf, lambs' tongue etc.)
· 1 tomato, thinly sliced
· 2 very thin slices striploin steak
· sea salt and freshly ground black pepper

Cook onion in a small splash of oil in a pan until soft and golden. While that's happening, smear bread with mustard one side only. Lay lettuce leaves and tomato slices on one piece. Season steak generously with freshly ground black pepper. Remove onions from pan and reserve. Add a little more oil to pan and heat until smoking. Add the steak, searing well to brown on each side, but leaving it still pink and juicy within. Pop onto leaves, season with a little salt, and finish with onions and remaining slice of bread, mustard side down, on top.

Fried Eggs, Parma Ham and Golden Tomato Bread

This gives new meaning to the words 'fry-up'! Choose best free range eggs, wafer-thin Italian parma ham. The bread is fried golden in olive oil, to provide the best soldiers for dipping in the egg yolk.

Serves 4

· light olive oil for frying
· 8 wafer thin slices parma ham
· 8 fingers tomato bread or good French bread
· 4 fresh free range eggs
· 2 tbsp sunflower oil

Heat a little olive oil in a heavy bottomed non-stick pan and fry the parma ham slices until crisp. Remove, blot on kitchen paper, and reserve, keeping hot. Add more oil to pan, then when its hot, add the fingers of tomato bread (the oil should sizzle as the bread goes in). Fry until bases are golden, then turn over to cook other sides. Blot these on kitchen paper too, and reserve with ham. In a clean pan, fry eggs in sunflower oil, keeping the yolks soft. Serve an egg and a couple of slices of crispy ham on each plate, with the tomato bread soldiers on the side.

Rare Roast Beef on Rye

A great way to use up a bit of leftover roast rib of beef. But make no mistake. I'd go out and buy a small piece of fillet to cook specially for these sandwiches. A big platter makes a terrific Sunday brunch dish.

MAKES 1

· 2 slices best rye bread
  – whatever thickness
  you fancy!
· 1–2 tsp creamed
  horseradish sauce
· few sprightly sprigs fresh
  watercress, rinsed and
  patted dry
· about 3 very thin slices rare
  roast beef
· 1 ripe tomato, thinly sliced

Smother the bread slices one side only with a decent amount of creamed horseradish, depending on how hot you like it. On one slice, lay the fresh watercress so it covers the horseradish generously. Ripple the thin slices of beef over that, so they overlap a little. Finish with the tomato slices and cover with the remaining piece of rye, horseradish side down.

Pain Tradition with Rocket, Brie and Cranberry Sauce

More than a touch of the 'Ooh-la-las!' about this concoction. It relies on perfectly ripe brie, which has been left out at room temperature for a while to give that oozy, just-beginning-to-run texture to the centre of the cheese. The cranberry sauce adds a bite of acidity to the mix, offsetting the rich creaminess in the cheese.

MAKES 1

· generous hunk of Pain
  Tradition
· unsalted butter (optional)
· baby rocket leaves
· few slivers of ripe brie
· 1–2 tsp cranberry sauce

Halve the bread horizontally and spread cut sides with butter if using it. Layer rocket on one half, then brie, then cranberry sauce, finishing with more rocket. Pop other half on top.

Smoked Salmon with Dill Sour Cream on Brown Soda

Traditional combo, granted – but one that never fails to please. These open sandwiches make a lovely first course or light lunch in the summer. Flavour the sour cream with chopped dill, or substitute snipped chives or finely sliced spring onion just as well.

Mix sour cream with dill, lemon zest and seasoning. Thinly butter the bread slices. Lay smoked salmon slices on top, folding them softly over one another so they look pretty. Season generously with freshly ground black pepper. Finish each with a spoon of the sour cream mix, in the centre of the salmon. Decorate with fresh sprigs of dill and thin wedges of lemon.

MAKES 4

· 4 tbsp sour cream
· 1 tbsp fresh chopped dill
· finely grated zest of a lemon
· sea salt and freshly ground black pepper
· 4 slices Irish brown soda bread
· little Irish butter for spreading
· 8 slices smoked salmon
· extra sprigs of dill and thin lemon wedges to finish

More Ideas for Bread

- Day-old sourdough makes great croutons for soup. Simply cut into fairly rustic-looking chunks, then shallow fry in hot sunflower oil, turning over with a spatula, until all the sides are golden and crisp. The secret of good croutons is to make sure the oil is hot first. Test it by throwing in a bread cube. It should sizzle straight away if it's ready.

- Use stale Pain Tradition (real French bread) for crumbs to coat chicken breast fillets. Carefully remove the crust, then crumb the remainder in a processor. Mix with chopped parsley, sea salt and freshly ground black pepper, crushed garlic and grated lemon zest. Coat skinless chicken breast fillets by first dipping in flour, then beaten egg, then the flavoured crumbs. Bake in a hot oven, Gas 5/375°F/190°C for 30 minutes or until chicken is cooked through and crumbs are golden and crisp.

- Garlic bread is easy to make with a crusty loaf of Pain Tradition. Normally, garlic bread is made with butter, but I prefer it with good extra virgin olive oil. Cut a whole baguette into about six chunks, then halve the chunks horizontally. Lay halves on a baking sheet. Brush the cut sides with a mix of 150ml/¼pt extra virgin olive oil, 4 peeled and crushed cloves garlic, 2 tbsp finely chopped parsley, sea salt and fresh ground black pepper. Bake in a hot oven, Gas 6/400°F/200°C for 10 minutes or until golden and crisp. Serve with pasta.

Norman, Veronica and Quinlan Steele – Cheesemakers

Ireland's Beara Peninsula was once remote and secluded, inhabited only by people who were born and reared in a landscape that challenged both resilience and resources. All that changed in the late 1960s and early 1970s, when the region began to attract the attention of those seeking a quiet lifestyle, and yearning to give up the demands of city living for a cottage by the sea. Norman Steele was one of them.

Today, this Professor of Philosophy and his wife, Veronica, live in an old farmhouse in Eyeries, on the Beara Peninsula, overlooking the waters of Coulagh Bay. On a clear day, they can stand in their back garden and admire the blue of the ocean and the purple green peaks of the Kerry mountains beyond. Spectacular is an understatement to describe the location of their home. Eyeries is a small village in Beara and, even though the entire region has seen a surge in home building since Norman first took residence all those years ago, it's still possible to get that feeling of being quite cut off from the rest of the world. Once the winding road swings right from the centre of the busy fishing village of Castletownbere, and cuts across the narrow strip of rocky headland to the opposite coastline, mobile phone contact is often lost and the car radio refuses to work in some places. Even for those who know the region well, the Beara still holds the appeal of isolation and solitude that first attracted Norman.

Conversation flows freely in the Steele household. Dublin-born Veronica leans up against the kitchen range and chats about cheese, life in West Cork and beyond, and any other topic that raises its head. The range is the same on which she first made Milleens some thirty years ago. Norman joins in the banter, seated at the kitchen table where a Milleens 'dote' is going unctuously gooey and wooing anyone that passes by. He tells of the birth of Ireland's first ever artisan farmhouse cheese so eloquently, mentioning in passing that 'When Jane

Grigson came here, she sat where you are.' Only then is it possible to grasp how monumentally influential these two have been on the modern Irish food scene. And it makes you go that bit runny in the middle. Just like their wonderful cheese.

English-born Norman studied philosophy at Trinity College, Dublin. After graduating, he went into lecturing, visiting the Beara during holidays. He fell in love with the place and the lifestyle and eventually gave up the city, and his job, for his first, tiny two-up two-down cottage in nearby Allihies. Settling into the relaxed pace of life, Norman forged a living rearing a few animals, growing some vegetables and making doors and window frames with a local carpenter. Then, quite out of the blue, he was asked to return to his educational profession to give a guest lecture. Fate took a hand when Veronica, a student of philosophy, attended. Soon she had moved to the tiny cottage, where the pair lived the country life. Eventually, the increase in livestock dictated a move to a farmhouse with more land in Eyeries. Norman kept pigs, cows, hens and ducks and grew vegetables to sustain their brood of four young children. It's a lifestyle many would seek out and, as Norman says, an 'idyllic way to raise a family.' All the Steele children grew up surrounded by animals, helping out on the farm, eating home-grown organic produce and spending time with mum and dad on long walks by the seashore.

The Steeles were the first artisan cheese producers in Ireland, discovered by Declan Ryan of Arbutus, then Myrtle Allen. Milleens came about, says Norman, 'as a result of too much milk from our cows'. Veronica began utilizing the excess for cheese. She made lots of different ones. One day, in 1976, she made Milleens. And history. Of its rise to fame, Norman says

> 'Veronica had started making the cheese, and gave some to a friend of ours. But instead of eating it, she put it on the menu in her restaurant. Quite coincidentally, Declan Ryan, then the chef owner of Arbutus Lodge, was eating there that night. He loved it and wanted to know more about who had made it. From there, Myrtle Allen got to hear of it and it was on the menu in Ballymaloe House before long.'

This quietly spoken gentleman genuinely puts the rise to fame of Milleens down to the fact that there was nothing else like it at the time, so it didn't need the aid of a whirl of publicity. Whilst that is certainly true, it must be remembered that its appeal has endured through 30 years of production, still in the same farmhouse with the same methods, and its special character and flavour has earned it

Milleens Tasting Notes

This simple, rustic washed-rind farmhouse cheese comes in large or small rounds fondly named 'dotes' by Veronica. It needs a little time out of the fridge before serving to allow the texture to soften and become slightly squidgy in the centre. Then, the fragrance and flavours of fresh herbs, wild mushrooms and creamy milk really come to the fore. Enjoy it with plain or wholemeal crackers, or a good hunk of crusty bread. Milleens loves red wine – so choose a Fleurie from Beaujolais, or perhaps a red from Navarra in northern Spain, which has a touch of spicy Tempranillo in the blend.

numerous accolades all over the world. It has proved itself as one of this country's most loved and best-quality local foods, still riding high in the popularity stakes with Ireland's top chefs, and gracing the shelves of prestigious cheesemongers, such as Sheridan's in Dublin and Neal's Yard, London.

Veronica Steele has long hung up her pinny and handed her cheese-making expertise on to son Quinlan, whom she says is even more passionate about getting it right than her. That's some praise from a woman who experimented and dabbled with many cheese styles before taking two years to perfect the Milleens' recipe and washed-rind technique that is so much a part of its long standing success. While she made cheese, Norman carried on milking cows, having to seek out extra supplies when demand for her creation increased far beyond what either of them could have ever imagined. Some years into production, after the BSE crisis hit Ireland, the Steeles gave up their herd in favour of getting all the milk from a group of local farmers. 'By then, we weren't producing enough for what we needed anyway', explains Norman. It meant he could devote himself full time to distribution, a task he still takes on for shops in the immediate locality.

Quinlan Steele is a chip off the old block. His mother is absolutely right when she says he is consumed with passion for his subject. This young, self-motivated second-generation cheesemaker grew up, like his siblings, fetching cows, helping to milk, and watching on as his parents created a speciality food now synonymous with this part of Ireland. He spends every day working at achieving perfection in his product. And, though the family herd has long gone, Quinlan still knows every one of the cows on the local farms which produce milk specially for him. Milleens is a soft, washed-rind cheese, with a creamy, mushroomy character he puts down to the 'diversity of the grazing in the Beara, and the uniqueness of the bacteria that settles on the rind, adding a special touch to the finished product.'

Milleens cheeses are young, some ready for eating after just 16 days. The milk is pasteurized, and curds set with rennet to a soft, tofu-like texture in around an hour. Quinlan handles them as delicately as possible when transferring to the moulds. Brined cheeses are left in the curing room to mature. Each day, he brings out just a few cheeses at a time from the curing room and brushes their rinds gently, rather like an artist adding the final brushstrokes to a painting. This is what encourages those precious bacteria, giving the orange pink hue to the rind, the pale creaminess to the texture, and that rich, leafy, lactic flavour. When ready to eat, Milleens is invitingly soft, yet jumping wth taste. Leave it out at room temperature for a while, and it becomes seductively oozy, throwing out tempting snatches of its characteristic woodland aromas all over the kitchen.

Norman and Veronica Steele have taught many their craft since starting the artisan cheese movement all those years ago. Many a cheese-making wannabe has joined them round the kitchen table in Eyeries, hoping to glean just a fraction of the knowledge, an ounce of the dedication and commitment for which these two are lauded. Now, with son Quinlan at the helm, Ireland's first ever farmhouse cheese greets a new era. And it goes on.

Tomato and Milleens Risotto

Milleens is one of those cheeses that works as well in cooking as on the cheese board. Its luxurious texture adds creaminess to risotto, which must be rich and yielding to be anything like as good as it should. When using Milleens, you don't need to add the usual extra knob of butter at the end of making the risotto to give the desired consistency. The cheese does it for you. Just one thing though. Keep it in the fridge until ready to use, or it'll come to life and start crawling out of its rind in the warmth of the kitchen. That's exactly the desired effect when putting it on the cheeseboard. But try cutting it like that!

Heat butter and oil in a pan and fry onion and garlic until soft but not browned. Stir in rice to coat with the mix. When it's coated with the oniony bits, add a ladle of stock. Bring to bubbling and let it absorb before adding another ladle. Continue like this until half the stock is incorporated. Stir in tomato flesh and continue adding remaining stock gradually until rice is tender. The consistency should be creamy but not too runny, so add more or less stock as required. Stir in Milleens to melt. Season and add lemon juice. Sprinkle in fresh snipped chives to finish. Serve in warmed bowls, with a little more Milleens for the top and some whole chives to decorate.

SERVES 4

· knob of butter
· 1 tbsp sunflower oil
· 1 onion, peeled and finely chopped
· 2 cloves garlic, peeled and crushed
· 275g/10oz arborio rice (risotto rice)
· 850ml/1½pt vegetable or chicken stock, approx.
· 225g/8oz fresh tomatoes, skinned, seeded and chopped
· 100g/4oz Milleens, rind removed
· sea salt and freshly ground black pepper
· squeeze of lemon juice
· 1 tbsp fresh snipped chives
· extra slivers of Milleens for the top
· whole chives for decoration

Broccoli Soup with Milleens

Fresh broccoli is normally married with cheddar in designer soups. I've used Milleens for a change and it creates a bowlful worthy of a smart dinner party first course. For delicacy, serve it in china soup bowls with handles, which bring an old-fashioned touch of refinement to the table.

Prepare the broccoli by chopping off the heads and separating into florets, then trimming and chopping the stalks. (The stalks have heaps of flavour so use them!) Heat oil in a pan and fry onion and garlic until soft but not browned. Add potato and cook for another few minutes, stirring gently. Don't allow the potato to brown. Pour over stock and bring to bubbling. Cover and simmer until potato is almost tender. Add broccoli and cook for about five minutes, or until everything is tender. Stir in knobs of Milleens then transfer soup to a processor and whiz smooth. Return to pan and reheat gently, seasoning with salt and freshly ground black pepper. Pour into bowls and decorate with a swirl of cream if you like, and chopped parsley.

SERVES 4

· 450g/1lb fresh broccoli
· 2 tbsp sunflower oil
· 1 onion, peeled and finely chopped
· 1 clove garlic, peeled and crushed
· 1 medium potato, peeled and in small chunks
· 1.1l/2pt vegetable stock
· 75g/3oz Milleens, rinded weight, in small knobs
· sea salt and freshly ground black pepper
· fresh cream (optional) and 1 tbsp finely chopped parsley for decoration

Milleenoise Potatoes

This is similar to Gratin Dauphinoise, but with the addition of egg to give a more set consistency. Slivers of Milleens tucked in between the layers add a special flavour to the finished dish. Blanching the potato slices first helps the cooking along. This is delicious as an accompaniment to a roast leg of lamb.

Blanch potatoes in lightly salted water for a few minutes. Drain and pat dry in a clean tea towel. Rub a large ovenproof gratin dish with butter and layer potatoes in it in an attractive, overlapping pattern. Add slivers of Milleens here and there, and season between layers. Beat eggs with cream and season. Pour over and dot top with extra Milleens. Bake at Gas 5/375°F/190°C for 45 minutes or until tender and golden. Cover the top with foil if it becomes too brown as it's cooking.

SERVES 4

· 900g/2lb largish potatoes, peeled and cut into thick slices

· 25g/1oz butter, softened

· 100g/4oz Milleens, rinded and in slivers

· sea salt and freshly ground black pepper

· 4 fresh free range eggs

· 300ml/½pt cream

· extra slivers of Milleens for top

Gourmet Cheeseburgers

Burgers are not all bad! If you make them properly from fresh ingredients, and serve on good crusty rolls, they are what real fast food is all about. These ones use lamb, spiked with a little chilli and flavoured with fresh oregano. If you can't get oregano, use coriander or parsley instead. Top them with the Milleens, then flash under a hot grill so it melts enticingly on top. Delicious!

Mix mince with garlic, onion, chilli and oregano. Season generously with salt and freshly ground black pepper. Add lemon juice and zest, and enough egg to bind. Work together with hands to mix well. Nip off a tiny piece, and fry quickly in a little hot oil to test for seasoning. Add more if necessary. Form remaining mix into 6 small burgers or 4 larger ones. Brush with oil and grill for about 8 minutes each side depending on thickness, or until meat juices show no signs of pinkness. Top with Milleens slices and flash under the grill for a few seconds to melt. Serve on crunchy rolls with lettuce, tomatoes, sliced baby gherkins and chutney.

SERVES 4

· 700g/1½lb best lamb mince
· 2 cloves garlic, peeled and crushed
· ½ onion, peeled and grated
· pinch dried red chilli flakes (optional)
· 1 tbsp fresh finely chopped oregano
· salt and freshly ground black pepper
· juice and zest of half a lemon
· 1 egg, beaten, to bind
· sunflower oil for brushing
· 100g/4oz Milleens, sliced
· toasted ciabatta crunchy rolls, lettuce, tomato slices, baby gherkins and fruit chutney to serve

Red Pepper and Cheese Breads

These griddle-softened red pepper pieces are served on warm, toasted baguette slices drizzled with olive oil, soft Milleens and fresh basil. In summer, fire up the barbie and cook the peppers on that for a charcoal-infused flavour, then serve these breads as a first course while everything else is cooking. A note about the cheese. It needs to be slightly soft to serve but be careful it doesn't get too runny. The heat of the bread will soften it more.

SERVES 4

- 2 long red sweet peppers
- extra virgin olive oil
- sea salt and freshly ground black peppers
- 2 baguette rolls
- 100g/4oz Milleens, left to soften slightly before cutting
- few fresh basil leaves

Halve peppers and scrape out seeds. Drizzle with olive oil and season. Heat a griddle pan until smoking then add peppers, or cook over hot barbecue coals until softened and charred, turning over to cook both sides evenly.

Meanwhile, halve rolls horizontally. Toast both sides, either on the pan, over the coals or conventionally. Keep warm. When peppers are softened, drizzle bread with a little olive oil. Lay slices of Milleens on top then finish with half a pepper and fresh basil leaves. Season and serve with a green salad.

More Ideas for Milleens

- In summer, grab some fresh organic salad leaves from a local farmers' market, or better still, grow them yourself outdoors under the protection of a small glass vegetable frame, and serve them with warm crispy bacon and small chunks of Milleens cheese. For a real culinary experience, make sure the bacon is dry cure, preferably free range, in either loin or streaky, chopped in large pieces and cooked crisp. This fresh-tasting salad needs only a simple vinaigrette of 1 tbsp white wine vinegar, 4 tbsp extra virgin olive oil, ½ tsp Dijon mustard, sea salt and freshly ground black pepper. Sprinkle over the leaves in a large bowl, then add the bacon and cheese and toss.

- Stuff upturned caps of large field mushrooms with slices of Milleens then cover with garlic and parsley breadcrumbs. Drizzle with melted butter, and bake in a hot oven until the crumbs are golden and the mushrooms are tender, covering the dish with foil if they get too coloured before they are ready.

- On the cheeseboard, Milleens works really well with fresh cherries or ripe fresh apricots which really enhance its gorgeous, creaminess and herbaceous, woodland flavours.

Eve St Leger –
Expert Chocolatier

Theobroma cacao, the botanical name for the cacao tree whose beans make chocolate, means 'food for the gods'. Those gods knew only too well the pleasure-giving qualities of one of the most sensual foods Mother Nature ever invented. Cacao beans contain caffeine and theobromine, stimulants that can have an aphrodisiac effect. Perhaps that's why most would agree good chocolate is very, very sexy.

The word 'chocolate' derives from 'chocolatl', – a combination of the Maya and Aztec tongues which means 'hot water'. Both these ancient races drank ground cacao dissolved in hot water – the original hot chocolate. Europe's first introduction to the substance came through Columbus, then Hernando Cortes, who conquered the Aztecs and took their dark and delicious secret to Spain. In the process of making chocolate, cacao beans must first be dried, fermented, roasted then ground so their fat – that all important cocoa butter – becomes liquid. Best-quality chocolate has a high cocoa butter (or cocoa solids) content of at least 70 per cent.

Among the units of an industrial estate on the edge of Cork city – the intense 'come hither' aroma of finest chocolate lingers on the air. Its presence is almost tangible, its allure irresistible. The scent gives away the location of one of Ireland's most exclusive chocolate boutiques, owned by Cork city-born Eve St Leger. This expert chocolatier embraced the magic of the dark stuff over a decade ago, and its spell has never worn off.

A self-confessed passion for good food led to a career change for this one-time office administrator – and with it – the start of a long relationship with chocolate. 'I love cooking and live to eat. I always knew deep down I wanted to do something in food.' Creating beautiful artisan chocolates was it, and Eve began by learning the practicalities of the trade from the world's experts before branching into her own business. She spent time in Switzerland, home of

superlative chocolate, perfecting her art under the watchful guidance of some of the most acclaimed Master Chocolatiers in the industry.

After intense training, Eve finally returned to her home turf bursting with inspiration, and set about building a home kitchen from which to work on the development of chocolates made to her own recipes. Her aim was to create a distinctive range of top-class chocolates specially suited to the Irish market. 'I knew exactly the sort of chocolates I wanted to make, using only luxury ingredients and incorporating the subtle sweetness that suits Irish tastes', she explains. Her commitment was the key to success and pretty soon she had built a stream of regulars who were supplied from the small, home-based business. Increased demand brought with it the need for a larger work space and, inevitably, five years later, a move to her present premises on the edge of the city.

Eve's Chocolate Shop, which she runs with the help of brother Guy, is a little piece of paradise, a gem that twinkles like a diamond in the rough of its workaday surroundings. An industrial estate is the most unexpected place to find a treasure trove of chocoholic fantasies. But those in the know come here from home and abroad to buy from the magnificent selection of handmade confectionary, and just to indulge in the pure, hedonistic pleasure of spending time here. If the Prince of Darkness really does exist, he most certainly resides among the boxes, bags and sparkly paper-wrapped indulgences. In fact, he even plays a part in the packaging design. Eve's striking black and white logo features a fig leaf and the phrase 'A little temptation'.

Eve's Chocolate Collection

Handmade plain, milk and white chocolate truffles with a selection of fillings. Corkies, Eve's famous nut and chocolate clusters, Branchelli fingers, slogan bars, cooking and drinking chocolate, sugar confectionary, nougat and traditional boiled sweets. Seasonal specialities.

An enclosed area at the far end of the shop houses the small kitchen where only the chosen few enter. In this inner sanctum, Eve devises recipes and experiments in creating chocolates from superlative ingredients. 'I use best quality, full fat Irish butter, milk and cream. And if you do that, you should get it right.' Her stunning fresh cream truffles, praised by food critics and professional chefs, have won many well-deserved plaudits, including being named Ireland's best handmade truffles by the Irish Food Writers Guild at the Chocolate Lovers Awards held in 2004. A glass-fronted, refrigerated cabinet under the shop counter displays these award-winning, reputation-making delicacies – Cointreau, Irish Whiskey, Champagne, and delightful White Chocolate truffles stand proudly to attention beside divine Dark Chocolate truffles, some coconut-capped, as if frosted by a light sprinkling of snow. All crook a seductive, beckoning finger at their admirers. They come hand-packed to order, and it's many a customer who falters in the choosing. The overwhelming urge to eat one straight away, perfectly chilled so the thick chocolate-coated exterior cracks sensuously between the teeth, is nigh on impossible to resist. A love affair with these truffles lasts forever.

It's difficult to know where to feast your eyes in a shop where every shelf heaves with hand-crafted creations of one kind or another. Chunky slogan and message bars in plain or milk chocolate shout bold greetings in twirly white chocolate handwriting. A box of chocolate-covered clusters of caramel and nuts, specially named 'Corkies' after Eve's beloved home city, attract attention from born and bred Corkonians and visitors alike. High on an upper shelf, rows of gilt-edged cellophane jewel pouches bulge with stashes of teeny chocolate nibs, made for melting into hot milk for a luxury take on the drink those Aztecs raved about. Not much beats a steaming mug of this for warming the cockles on a cold day. After a long winter walk, enjoy it even better with a small shot of cognac stirred through and some soft pink and white marshmallows floating on top.

Patisserie chefs, professional confectioners and enthusiastic home cooks know the importance of good chocolate when it comes to making the best cakes, desserts and mousses. Eve's cooking chocolate comes in coin-sized discs, which melt easily into a smooth, creamy pool for folding or stirring into the chosen recipe. The dark plain chocolate has 72 per cent cocoa solids, well over the 70 per cent minimum essential for cooking; milk chocolate has 34 per cent cocoa solids, and the white, one of the most difficult to get right, has 28 per cent. Eve St Leger is a mistress of black magic who has devoted herself to crafting some of the finest handmade chocolates in this country. Buying them is definitely up there among life's best retail therapy treats. Eating them? Welcome to the Pleasure Dome.

Profiteroles with Chocolate Sauce

Classic dessert of choux pastry buns, filled with cream, and drizzled with fresh chocolate sauce. Eve St Leger makes her own so try and get your hands on some if you can. Choux pastry is easily made and suited to those who are not generally good pastry makers. After the initial cooking, these little buns need about ten minutes or so at a slightly lower temperature to dry out the insides and make them crisp. For a special occasion gathering, make them in double quantity and stack in a pyramid on a stylish cake stand, with the sauce dripping down.

MAKES ABOUT 20 SMALL PROFITEROLES

· 150ml/¼pt water
· 50g/2oz butter
· 65g/2½oz plain flour
· pinch of salt
· 2 fresh free range eggs
· 150ml/¼pt cream, whipped to soft peaks
· 1 tub dark chocolate sauce

Place water and butter in a pan and bring to the boil. Sift flour and salt together onto a sheet of greaseproof then tip it all in the pan of boiling water and butter at once. Beat vigorously with a wooden spoon until all is incorporated and dough leaves the sides of the pan cleanly. Cool slightly, then gradually add eggs, one at a time beating in until mix is smooth and shiny. Spoon small balls onto a lightly oiled baking sheet. Bake in a preheated oven, Gas 5/375°F/190°C for 20 minutes or until pale golden and set. Lower heat to Gas 4/350°F/180°C for another 10 minutes or until crisp and dry. Remove and cool.

Pierce a small hole in each bun and pipe a little whipped cream inside. Pile on a serving platter. Heat chocolate sauce according to instructions, then drizzle over profiteroles before serving.

Chocolate Mousses

Little pots of extravagance, made from best-quality dark chocolate spiked with black coffee and brandy. They look stunning served in plain, white espresso coffee cups, but if you haven't got any, use small ramekins or glasses. The lactic acidity of the crème fraiche, which is used to decorate the mousses, just breaks through that richness of the chocolate for a balancing effect.

Melt chocolate with black coffee in a bowl over a pan of simmering water. Stir smooth. Remove from heat and cool slightly. Beat egg yolks with sugar until mix forms a trail. Fold into the chocolate mix with brandy. Whisk egg whites stiff and fold into mixture with a metal spoon. Divide between little ramekins or espresso coffee cups. Chill for at least 2 hours to set. Decorate with little mounds of crème fraiche with chopped chocolate on top.

SERVES 4–6 (DEPENDING ON WHAT YOU SERVE THEM IN)

· 225g/8oz 72 per cent dark chocolate, in disks or bars, broken into squares
· 2 tbsp strong black coffee
· 4 eggs, separated
· 2 tbsp caster sugar (or to taste)
· 1 tbsp of brandy
· crème fraiche and finely chopped dark chocolate for decoration

Rich Chocolate Cake

This recipe was invented by a foodie friend as was the shiniest chocolate sauce ever (see tips). It's inky dark and richly intense – hence the name – so you need only the merest sliver to be absolutely gratified. Serve thin slices with a little cream and some fresh raspberries or strawberries as an elegant pud. Make the presentation posh by popping the slivers and berries on large white plates and dusting the outside edges with cocoa powder passed through a small, fine sieve.

Melt chocolate in a bowl set over a pan of simmering water. Add butter and sugar and stir until melted and smooth. Remove from heat. Beat in egg yolks one at a time. Whisk egg whites stiff. Fold in half the whites with flour. Then carefully fold in the rest of the egg whites, being careful not to bash out all the air. Pour into a greased loose-bottomed 20cm/8″ cake tin, the base lined with a disc of greaseproof. Bake in a preheated oven, Gas 4/350°F/ 180°C for 45 minutes or until cake is firm but still a little soft to the touch in the very middle. Cool slightly in tin then turn out and cool completely on a wire rack.

For the icing, melt chocolate with cream in a pan and add add butter cubes. Stir smooth then cool. Peel greaseproof from base of cake, and set on a large flat plate or cake board. Spoon over icing and let it run down the sides. It doesn't matter if it pools in places on the plate. Leave in a cool place to set. Decorate with chocolate curls (see later). Serve in thinnest slivers with the berries on the side, and cream if you wish.

Serves about 10

- Makes a 20cm/8″ cake
- 350g/12oz best dark chocolate (at least 70 per cent cocoa solids)
- 175g/6oz unsalted butter, in small chunks
- 175g/6oz caster sugar
- 5 free range eggs, separated
- 50g/2oz plain flour

For the icing:
- 175g/6oz best dark chocolate
- 100ml/4floz cream
- 15g/½oz butter
- fresh raspberries or strawberries, and cream, for serving

Boozy Chocolate Trifle

This hits the spot every time, utilizing the best in convenience ingredients to create a graceful finale for any celebration menu. Chocolate muffins provide a moist, cakey base for canned black cherries, melted dark chocolate and liqueur, and generous layers of custard and whipped cream. The cheat's custard is easy peasy – enriched with thick, creamy West Cork crème fraiche. This trifle should be made in a clear glass bowl – preferably not cut crystal, to show off all those lovely layers and textures.

Mix custard powder with 2 tbsp milk to a smooth paste. Bring remaining milk to just under bubbling, whisk on to paste then return to pan. Whisk over low heat to thicken. Sweeten to taste. Remove, place in a bowl, cover surface with film to prevent it skinning over, then cool.

Place half muffin slices in a large glass bowl. Drizzle over half the liqueur, scatter over half the cherries and spoon on a third of the melted chocolate. Layer remaining muffin slices and drizzle with remaining liqueur, top with cherries and another third of the melted chocolate. Leave this to rest for a while. Mix cooled custard with crème fraiche until smooth and spoon over. Smooth surface. Chill for 30 minutes or until ready to serve. Spread whipped cream over custard, then scatter with toasted almond flakes. Finally drizzle with remaining melted chocolate and serve.

SERVES 6

· 2 tbsp custard powder
· 425ml/¾pt milk
· sugar to taste
· 8–10 small chocolate chip muffins, sliced
· 50ml/2floz Bailey's Irish Cream liqueur (or more to taste)
· 2 x 400g cans pitted black cherries, drained
· 100g/4oz best dark chocolate, (at least 70 per cent cocoa solids) melted
· 200ml/7floz crème fraiche
· 300ml/½pt cream, whipped
· toasted flaked almonds for decoration

Party Pavlova

Great way to finish a meal, this looks spectacular and tastes spectacular! I make this in winter and use festive mandarin oranges as part of the fruit topping. But in summer, substitute these with fresh strawberries. The brown sugar gives the meringue base a delicious, toffee fudginess. Make it in advance and store in an airtight tin.

Whisk egg whites in a bowl until stiff. Whisk in 2 tbsp sugar until mix is glossy. Carefully fold in remaining sugar with a metal spoon. Spoon in a circle onto a baking sheet lined with non-stick baking parchment. Cook in a preheated oven Gas ½/75°F/140°C for 1½ hours or until dried out and crisp. Turn off heat and leave meringue inside to cool completely.

Whip cream to thick peaks with Bailey's and icing sugar. Peel baking parchment from base of meringue then pop on a serving plate. Spoon whipped cream all over. Arrange fruit on top and drizzle melted chocolate over.

SERVES 4–6

- 4 egg whites
- 225g/8oz golden demerara sugar
- 300ml/½pt cream
- 1 tbsp Bailey's Irish Cream liqueur
- 2 tsp icing sugar, sifted
- 1 ripe pineapple, peeled, cored and in wedges
- 2 mandarins, peeled and in segments
- 100g/4oz best dark chocolate (at least 70 per cent cocoa solids) melted

More Ideas for Eve's Chocolate

- Chocolate curls look spectacular on top of a cake or mousse. They aren't difficult to make after a bit of practice. Melt 100g/4oz best dark chocolate in a bowl over a pan of simmering water. Spread thinly onto a smooth-textured cool worktop (marble is perfect) or onto a marble cake board. Let the chocolate come almost to the point of resetting. Holding the blade of a cook's knife at an angle of about 45° degrees, slowly push it across the chocolate, scraping up the curls off the worktop and curling it as you go. As I said, it might need a few goes, but you will eventually get it right.

- Use best dark chocolate for a shiny chocolate sauce. Heat 150mls/¼pt water with 50g/2oz caster sugar, 1 tsp cocoa powder and 75g/3oz dark chocolate, stirring gently until smooth. Add another 150mls/¼pt water and bring to bubbling. Simmer for 15 minutes or until mix is slightly reduced, smooth and shiny. Serve warm or cold over ice cream or poached pears.

- Use the chocolate sauce above (or a tub of good ready-made sauce) for a dip for fresh strawberries, as a romantic dessert for two to share. Rinse the berries, patting dry carefully, but leave the calyxes intact to make it easy to pick up the fruits. Pour the sauce into a bowl and set in the centre of a platter. Surround with strawberries. Serve some pink champagne as well.

The Creators Directory

The Creators' Directory

This directory lists contact and produce details for all the Creators within these pages. A following list below gives details of other Cork producers.

From Land and Field

Caroline and Eddie Robinson
Page 15

Parkmore
Templemartin
Bandon
Tel: 021 7330178
Email: carolinerobinson@eircom.net

Fresh seasonal, chemical-free vegetables available from: *Macroom Market, West Cork, Tuesday mornings; Cornmarket Street Farmers' Market, Cork City, Saturdays; direct from the farm (telephone first).*

John Howard
Page 31

Sunnyside Fruit Farm
Rathcormac
County Cork
Tel: 025 36253
Email: sunnysidefruit@eircom.net

Selection of seasonal fresh berries, and home-grown frozen berries all year round. Available from: *Farm shop open 9–6pm in June, July and August. (Out of season, shop open Saturdays only. Telephone first.) Also Midleton Farmers' Market on Saturday mornings throughout the growing season.*

Eugene and Helena Hickey
Page 45

Skeaghanore Ducks and Geese
Skeaghanore
Ballydehob
West Cork
Tel: 028 37428
Email: skeaghanoreduck@eircom.net

Skeaghnore Ducks and Geese are West Cork Fuchsia branded. Sold whole or portioned in vacuum packs. Available from: *O'Donovan's Butchers, Princes Street and Wilton, Cork; Anthony O'Sullivan, Ballincollig, Cork; Mike Murphy, Turners Cross, Cork; Field's SuperValu, Skibbereen and Martin Carey Butchers, Bandon, West Cork. Frank Krawcyzk's stall, Bandon Farmers' Market, Saturdays. Also direct from farm (telephone first). Early ordering for Christmas geese essential.*

Madeline McKeever
Page 59

Ardagh Organic Beef and Brown
Envelope Seeds
Ardagh
Church Cross
Skibbereen
West Cork
Tel: 028 38184

Selection of beef cuts available from: *Direct from the farm (telephone first).* More information on seed saving available from Irish Seed Savers Association (Tel: 061 921866).

Willie and Avril Allshire
Page 75

Caherbeg Free Range Pork
Caherbeg
Rosscarbery
Tel: 023 48474
Fax: 023 48966
Email: caher@caherbegfreerangepork.ie

Fresh pork, pre-packed handmade
sausages, black and white puddings,
vacuum-packed dry cure bacon joints,
rashers and hams available from:
Martin Carey Butchers, Bandon, Caherbeg
and Rosscarberry Recipe sausages and bacon
from Field's SuperValu, Skibbereen and other
selected SuperValu stores. Angus beef
cuts also available direct from farm
(telephone first).

From the Waters

Sally Barnes
Page 95

Woodcock Smokery
Gortabrack
Castletownshend
West Cork
Tel: 028 36232
Email: sallybarnes@iolfree.ie

Woodcock Smokery products are
vacuum packed and West Cork Fuchsia
branded. Available from: *Good food shops*
throughout West Cork, Field's SuperValu,
Skibbereen. Telephone for Dublin and UK
stockists and mail order service.

Cornie Bohane
Page 111

Superlative selection of Cornie's freshly
caught fish and shellfish available from:
Daily auction at Union Hall Fisherman's
Co-op, Skibbereen (trade only); Alan
Hassett's Baltimore Fresh Fish stall,
Clonakilty Farmers' Market, Thursdays
and Bandon Farmers' Market, Saturdays.

Frank Hederman
Page 125

Belvelly Smokehouse
Belvelly
Cobh
East Cork
Tel: 021 481 1089
Email: shipping@frankhederman.com
or visit www.frankhederman.com

Selection of vacuum-packed Belvelly
Smokehouse Products available from:
Midleton Market, Saturday mornings;
English Market, Cork City; Mahon Point
Farmers' Market, Cork City, Thursdays;
and direct from Belvelly Smoke House.
Also from Harvey Nichols, London, UK.

Colin Whooley
Page 143

Ocean Run
Roaring Water Bay
County Cork
Tel: 086 248 3863

Rope-grown fresh mussels available in
pre-weighed nets from: *Alan Hassett's*
Baltimore Fresh Fish at Bandon Farmers'
Market, Scally's SuperValu; Clonakilty;
other selected local outlets. Also supplies to
order for restaurants throughout the region.
Telephone orders taken.

N.B. Driftnet ban in Ireland:
A ban on driftnet fishing for wild
salmon has now been introduced in
Ireland, taking effect from the 2007
season, which prevents commercial
fisherman from catching the fish out
at sea that are returning to Irish rivers
during the breeding season. It has been
introduced in order to combat the
decline in numbers of salmon returning
to this country, as recorded in recent
years. However, wild salmon can still be
caught with draft nets at river estuaries,
but only on those Irish rivers where
stock levels are deemed high enough to
be sustainable.

Special Delicacies

Anthony Creswell
Page 165

Ummera Smoked Products
Inchybridge
Timolegue
County Cork
Tel: 023 46644/ 087 2027227
Fax: 023 46419
Email: info@ummera.com
or visit www.ummera.com

Selection of vacuum-packed smoked fish, chicken and bacon, silver eels and Gravadlax. West Cork Fuchsia branded. Available from: *Cork: Martin Carey Butchers, Bandon; Field's SuperValu, Skibbereen; Kinsale; Gourmet Store, Kinsale; Manning's Emporium, Ballylicky, Bantry; Mangetout, Kinsale; Lettercollum Kitchen Project Shop, Clonakilty; On The Pig's Back, English Market; Scally's SuperValu, Clonakilty; The Douglas Hide Food Company, Carrigaline and Wilton; The Organic Shop, Clonakilty and English Market; Urru Culinary Store, Bandon; West Cork Gourmet Store, Schull. Dublin: Avoca Shops; Butler's Pantry Shops; Fallon and Byrne, Exchequer Street; Mortons of Ranelagh; Nolans' of Clontarf; Olive Delicatessen, Skerries; The Purty Kitchen Gourmet Shop, Dun Laoghaire. London: Mortimer and Bennett, Chiswick, Mr Christians Camden Passage, Islington, N1 and Elgin Crescent, Notting Hill Gate; Silver Side, Clifton Road, Maida Vale; The Food Hall, Old Street EC1; Trinity Stores, Balham, SW12.* Telephone or check the website for mail order.

Tom, Giana and Fingal Ferguson
Page 181

Gubbeen Farmhouse Products
Gubbeen House
Schull
County Cork
Tel: 028 27824 (Smokehouse)
Email: smokehouse@eircom.net
Tel: 028 28231
Fax: 028 28609
Email: gubbeencheese@eircom.net

Gubbeen Cheese comes in waxed rounds in plain and oak-smoked versions. Gubbeen Farmhouse Products are West Cork Fuchsia branded. Available from: *Iago and On the Pig's Back, English Market, Cork City; Manning's Emporium Ballylickey, Bantry; West Cork Gourmet Store, Schull; Urru Culinary Store, Bandon; Field's SuperValu, Skibbereen; Scally's SuperValu, Clonakilty and other selected SuperValu stores around the county. Also Superquinn, Dublin and Sheridan's cheesemongers, Dublin. Smokehouse products can be purchased at the Farmers' Markets in Skibbereen Saturdays and Kinsale Tuesday mornings, and direct from Fingal Ferguson at the above numbers.*

Bill Hogan and Sean Ferry
Page 199

West Cork Natural Cheese Company
Deereenatra
Schull
West Cork
Tel: 028 28593
Email: bh@wcnc.ie

Desmond and Gabriel Cheeses come in whole rounds, or individual pieces packed and sealed in waxed paper. West Cork Fuchsia branded. Available from: *Iago and On the Pig's Back, English Market, Cork; Manning's Emporium Ballylickey, Bantry; West Cork Gourmet Store, Schull; Urru Culinary Store, Bandon and other specialist Cork delis, Sheridan's Cheesemongers, Dublin; Superquinn, Dublin; Neal's Yard, London, UK.*

Declan Ryan
Page 215

Arbutus Breads
Unit 2B
Mayfield Industrial and Scientific Park
Mayfield
Cork
Tel: 021 450 5820/ 086 251 3919
Email: arbutus@iol.ie

Selection of Arbutus Breads available
from: *Urru Culinary Store, Bandon; On
the Pig's Back, English Market, Cork;
O'Herlihy's Artisan Shop, St. Luke's
Cross, Cork. Farmers' markets at Bantry,
Ballincollig, Cobh, Douglas, Midleton
and Mahon Point, Cork (see penultimate
section for listing of these markets).
Outside Cork: Kenmare, Dingle and Ennis.*

Norman, Veronica and Quinlan Steele
Page 227

Milleens Cheese
Milleens
Eyeries
Beara
County Cork
Tel: 027 74079
Fax: 027 74379
Email: info@milleenscheese.com

Milleens soft-washed rind cheeses come
in 1.6 kg rounds and small 'Dotes' at
200g. Available from: *Selected shops and
delis nationwide, local shops and delis in
West Cork; some SuperValu stores in the
county; On the Pig's Back, English
Market, Cork City; Sheridan's
Cheesemongers, Dublin.*

Eve St Leger
Page 241

Flair Confectionary
Eve's Chocolate Shop
College Commercial Park
Magazine Road
Cork
Tel: 021 434 7781
Email: eve@iol.ie

Eve's truffles can be bought loose by
weight, or pre-packed in varying sizes of
presentation boxes. Other confectionary
sold pre-packed, depending on product.
Available from: *The shop and mail
order by phone. Shop hours, 9:30–6pm,
Monday–Friday.*

More Producers in Cork

Fruit and Vegetables

David and Denise Bushby

Inchinattin
Rosscarbery
County Cork
Tel: 023 38140

The coastal area around Rosscarbery in West Cork is home to strawberry growers David and Denise Bushby. Their beautiful fruits are often the first to make an appearance in local shops and markets in mid-April, and last through to September. If you are in the area, a punnet of these spectacular scarlet fruits is definitely worth seeking out. Available from: *Hosford's Garden Centre, Enniskeane; Urru Culinary Store, Bandon and other local outlets.*

Breda Grinsell

Gairdin Eden
Edencurra
Dunmanway
County Cork
Tel: 023 45064/086 1963687
Fax: 023 45064

Breda grows a superb selection of organic salad leaves which she sells in mixed bags, plus potted organic herbs, such as thyme, sage, bronze fennel, sweet fennel and parsley. West Cork Fuchsia branded. Available from: *Bandon Farmers' Market, Saturdays; Fehily's Food Store, Ballineen; Urru Culinary Store, Bandon; and other local outlets.*

James and Catherine Higgins

Ballycotton Vegetables
Ballycotton
County Cork
Tel: 087 698 6227

The Higgins grow main crop and new potatoes, broccoli, cauliflowers, carrots, swedes, crisp outdoor lettuces, baby beetroots, etc. Available from: *Bandon Farmers' Market, Saturdays, Ballincollig Farmers' Market, Wednesdays; and their own outlet at The Country Garden Fruit and Vegetable Shop, Ballincurra, Midleton, County Cork.*

Rupert Hugh Jones
Ballymaloe Cookery School Organic
Farm and Gardens
Shanagarry
County Cork
Tel: 021 464 6785

Fresh vegetables in season, salads, etc;
organic herbs, free range eggs from the
farm and gardens of Ireland's famous
cookery school. Available from: *Own
shop at Ballymaloe; Midleton Farmers'
Market, Saturday mornings; Mahon Point
Farmers' Market, Thursdays.*

Declan, Trevor and Nigel Martin
Waterfall Farms Ltd
Ballyshoneen
Waterfall
Near Cork City
Tel: 021 487 0238
Fax: 021 487 4424
Email: wf@iol.ie

Convenient for the catering trade,
Waterfall Farm's prepared vegetables
come in vacuum packs, including
potatoes, single varieties or mixed
vegetable packs, stir fry, chowder
and ratatouille mixes, fresh fruit salad
and fresh herbs, whole home-grown
vegetables as well. West Cork Fuchsia
branded. Available from: *Farm
shop on the premises and own distribution
to catering establishments throughout Cork.*

Nick Moseley
Union Hall Fresh Produce
Union Hall
County Cork
Tel: 028 33609

Selected seasonal fruit and vegetables.
The summer strawberries are to die for,
and look for tender spinach leaves and
a variety of lettuces too. Available from:
*Farm shop, Field's SuperValu, Skibbereen;
Scally's SuperValu, Clonakilty; and small
independents in the locality.*

Willie Scannell
Ballycotton
County Cork
Tel: 021 464 6924

Willie grows a good varieties of
seasonal potatoes and other traditional
vegetables. Available from: *Direct from
the farm (telephone first) and Midleton
Farmers' Market, Saturday mornings.*

Poultry and Eggs

Dan and Ann Aherne
Aherne's Organic Farm,
Ballysimon,
Midleton
East Cork
Tel: 021 4631058/086 165 9258 (mobile)

Free range organic Born-Free chickens
reared on the family farm, sold as
whole birds or in portions. Also organic
beef and lamb cuts, depending on
stocks, home-made organic beefburgers
with fresh herbs and spices and free
range organic eggs. Available from:
*Scally's SuperValu, Clonakilty, West Cork;
Midleton Farmers' Market, Saturday
mornings. Direct from farm (telephone
first). Outside Cork: chickens from Nolan's
and Donnybrook Fayre in Dublin; Be
Organic, Donegal.*

James and Mary O'Brien
Valley View Free Range Eggs
Unit 6, Cloughmacsimon
Bandon
County Cork
Tel: 023 41173/ 43952
Fax: 023 41173
Email: vvfreerangeeggs@hotmail.com

James was the founder of the Irish
Free Range Egg Producers Association
(IFREPRA). All eggs produced on the
O'Brien's farm and specially selected
farms in the Bandon area.

Range includes Bord Bia quality assured free range eggs and free range mega eggs enriched with Omega 3. West Cork Fuchsia branded. Available from: *Selected SuperValu and Centra Stores and small independent retailers throughout the Cork/Kerry region.*

Brendan Ross
Cotournix Quail
Droumdrastil
Dunmanway
County Cork
Tel: 087 206 5067

Fresh quails' eggs and whole peeled and cooked eggs preserved in vinegar, sold in jars. Available from: *Field's SuperValu, Skibbereen, Scally's SuperValu, Clonakilty, and other selected stores in the area; Martin Carey Butchers, Bandon, West Cork. Direct from the farm (telephone first).*

Smoked Produce

Sean and Siobhan Nolan
Union Hall Smoked Fish
Union Hall
County Cork
Tel: 028 33125
Fax: 028 33797
Email: nolanelman@hotmail.com

Smoked wild salmon and farmed salmon, plain and peppered smoked mackerel, kippers, smoked trout, barbecue salmon and fish pâtés. West Cork Fuchsia branded. Vacuum packed. Available from: *Caulfield's SuperValu, Riverview Shopping Centre, Bandon; Scally's SuperValu, Clonakilty, O'Donovan's Centra, Enniskeane, and other selected stores and independents throughout West Cork and Kerry. Nationwide through Superquinn and SuperValu/Centra.*

Fresh Meat and Meat Products

This listing features selected butchers some of whom rear and slaughter their own animals.

Michael Bresnan
English Market
Grand Parade
Cork City
Tel: 021 427 1119

Long-standing butchering family who produce their own beef and lamb and have slaughterhouse facilities. Various offal cuts also available. Bresnan's sister Katherine O'Mahony also has a stall in the market (Tel: 021 4270254).

Martin Carey
Martin Carey Butchers
82 South Main Street
Bandon
Tel: 023 42107
Fax: 023 43439

Martin hand makes a huge selection of award-winning sausages from traditional Cumberland and Lincolnshire to Pork and Apple, Spicy Lamb, Gluten-Free Toulouse made with the Allshires' free range pork, and curly cartwheels of Boerwurst. You name it. Martin is a member of the Association of Craft Butchers of Ireland, winning its award for Best Sausage in Ireland in 2006. West Cork Fuchsia branded. Available from: *Direct from the shop.*

Collins Brothers
Dunmanway and Ballineen
County Cork
Tel: 023 47860 (Ballineen),
023 45336 (Dunmanway)

Traditional butchers selling beef and lamb from their own farm, pork from local farmers, free range chickens all year and free range turkeys and geese at Christmas. They have their own slaughtering facilities which really adds to the consistently good quality. Home-cured low salt bacon and own black pudding and breakfast pork sausages too, along with a small selection of locally grown seasonal vegetables. The brothers work from the Dunmanway shop, with Michael Burgoyne at the helm in Ballineen. Phone orders taken.

Robert Kelleher
Ballinagree
Macroom
County Cork
Tel: 026 41831

Lamb farmer and expert Border Collie trainer Robert Kelleher specializes in mountain lambs which dine on hardy, aromatic grasses, wild herbs and heathers on the hills around his farmhouse. Lambs are born in March and April, slightly later than lowland-reared animals, and ready for the summer market. Most go for sale at the local mart, to supply butchers all over the country. But those in the know can buy whole lamb – ready for the freezer – direct from the farm.

Jack McCarthy
Main Street
Kanturk
County Cork
Tel: 029 50178

Family butcher specializing in home made dry cured bacon, black puddings and sausages, air-dried meats, pancetta and Polish Kielbasa sausages. Good quality meats from local farms too.

J. McCarthy
Main Street
Drimoleague
County Cork
Tel: 028 31763

Lovely small butcher's shop, in a village setting. Great quality meats from own farm and selected neighbouring farms.

Suppliers of the week are listed on the blackboard. A limited selection of locally grown vegetables also available.

Dan Molony
Molony's Meat Centre
South Main Street
Bandon
County Cork
Tel: 023 44206

Dan's superb quality beef is produced on the family farm, managed by his brother. The farm has its own slaughtering facilities and Dan believes in lengthy hanging so the meat develops real flavour and tenderness. Choose from fillet, sirloin or rump steak, stewing, braising and pot roasting cuts, and the most majestic ribs of beef on the bone.

O'Crualaoi The Butchers
Main Street
Ballincollig
County Cork
Tel: 021 487 1205

A previous winner of a prestigious Bridgestone Guide award for the good choice of fresh meats from own slaughterhouse, and home-prepared cooked meat products.

J. O'Flynn
36 Marlborough Street
Cork City
Tel: 021 427 5685

Traditional butcher with an array of fresh meats and home made sausages, bacon, etc. Winner of a Slow Food Ireland award in 2005.

A. O'Neill
English Market
Grand Parade
Cork City
Tel: 021 427 0535

Long-established butchers and
specialists in own home-made recipe
corned and spiced beef.

A. O'Reilly
English Market
Grand Parade
Cork City
Tel: 021 427 0925

Cork's famous tripe and home made
drisheen stall in the market – not to
be missed!

Edward Twomey Butchers
16 Pearse Street
Clonakilty
County Cork
Tel: 023 33365

The home of Clonakilty Black Pudding,
made famous by Edward Twomey,
and created from a recipe he found
scribbled on a bit of scrap paper, in the
back of what was Harrington's Butcher's
shop when he first bought the premises.
Sadly, Edward has now passed away,
and his fun-loving, larger-than-life
presence is sincerely missed by those
who knew him. Nevertheless, he lives
on in his wonderful, boldly flavoured
black pudding, peppery white pudding,
home-cured bacon and butcher's
sausages. A genuine hero of the food
world, Edward Twomey put the taste
of Clonakilty on the lips of food
lovers far and wide. Clonakilty meat
products available from: *The butcher's
shop in Clonakilty; many Supervalu stores
throughout Ireland; airport shops in Cork
and Dublin; selected branches of Dunnes
Stores nationwide. Stockists in London too.
Telephone for details.*

Speciality Foods

Sonia Bower
Sonia's Inner Pickle
Alandone
County Cork
Tel: 028 37840/ 086 3131362

Sonia Bower makes a fabulous range
of Carribbean-influenced pickles and
chutneys quite different to the norm.
Spicy chilli, fresh ginger and whole
cloves of garlic feature with exotic
spices such as nutmeg and cinnamon.
Fabulous with cheese or charcuterie.
Available from: *Urru Culinary Store,
Bandon; and various other delis and
selected independents in Cork.*

Mary Burns
Adrahan Farmhouse Cheese
Kanturk
County Cork
Tel: 029 78099

A semi-soft cows' milk cheese with
a punchy, lactic flavour. Wrapped in
distinctive blue and white greaseproof
with a picture of a farmhouse on the
front. Available from: *Selected SuperValu
stores, delis and small independents
throughout Cork; English Market, Cork
City; Sheridan's Cheesemongers Dublin
and Galway.*

Jeffa Gill
Durrus Cheese
Coomkeen
Durrus
Bantry
County Cork
Tel: 027 61100
Fax: 027 61017
Email: durruscheese@eircom.net or
visit www.durruscheese.com

Jeffa Gill was one West Cork's earliest
cheesemakers, starting in 1979 to
supplement the income of her
small dairy farm situated in the hills
overlooking Dunmanus Bay. Demand
soon outgrew milk supply, however

and she gave up farming in favour of making cheese full time. Unpasteurized milk for the world-famous rind-washed Durrus cheese is now supplied from local herds. West Cork Fuchsia branded. Mature and young cheeses come in 380g or 1.5kg rounds. Available from: *Urru Culinary Store, Bandon; West Cork Gourmet Store, Schull; selected SuperValu stores in West Cork; On the Pig's Back, English Market, Cork City; Sheridan's Cheesemongers, Dublin.*

Dan Hegarty
Hegarty's Farmhouse Cheddar
Church Road
Whitechurch
County Cork
Tel: 021 488 4238

This farmhouse cheese, made from the farm's own milk, is one of the best cheddars around. Smooth and creamy with typical, slightly flaky texture and a good clout of lingering pepperiness to the flavour, which comes with long maturing. Available from: *Urru Culinary Store, Bandon; On the Pig's Back and Iago, English Market, Cork City; Scally's SuperValu, Clonakilty; and other selected stores in Cork.*

Alan and Valerie Kingston
Glenilen Dairy
Gurteenihir
Drimoleague
County Cork
Tel: 028 31179
Website: www.glenilenfarm.com

Gorgeous natural and flavoured yoghurt, clotted cream, cottage cheese, delicious cheesecakes and desserts, and natural hand-made farmhouse butter with low salt content, all made with milk from the farm's own herd. Available from: *Centra, Drimoleague; Colm Donnellan's Eurospar, Old Market Garden Bandon; Scally's SuperValu, Clonakilty; Field's SuperValu, Skibbereen; and other selected SuperValu stores in Cork; Urru Culinary Store, Bandon; West Cork Gourmet Store, Schull.*

Frank Krawczyk
Krawczyk's West Cork Salamis
Derreenatra
Schull
County Cork
Tel: 028 28579
Email: frankk@oceanfree.net

Fine selection of handmade charcuterie from local free range and organic meats. Superb flavours to the air-dried salamis, while Frank's duck liver pâté and pork rillettes are exquisite. Available from: *Farmers' Markets in Bantry (Friday mornings and Midleton Saturdays). Urru Culinary Store, Bandon; On the Pig's Back, English Market, Cork City; West Cork Gourmet Store, Schull.*

Aaron McDonnell
Finders Inn
Nohoval
Oysterhaven
County Cork
Tel: 021 770737

Aaron McDonnell's home-cooked produce from the family restaurant is superb. Smooth chicken liver pâté, gutsy red cabbage salad, ratatouille, fruit and herb vinaigrettes and, in summer, the most sublime ice creams are just part of his repertoire. The restaurant is in a very scenic location and has an air of old world romance about it. Finder's Inn produce available from: *Colm Donnellan's Eurospar, Bandon.*

Brendan Murphy and Richard May
Travara Lodge
Courtmacsherry
County Cork
Tel: 023 46493

Travara Lodge's range of home-made speciality products includes unusual relishes, pestos, jams, preserves, soups, buns, cakes, bread and all sorts of goodies! The Lodge also does B&B. Available from: *Courtmacsherry Market, every Friday morning 10am–noon, The Chessboard on the Promenade, June, July and August only. Catering for private functions by request.*

Jane Murphy
Ardsallagh Goat's Products
Woodstock
Carrigtwohill
County Cork
Tel: 021 488 2336

Delicious soft goats' milk cheeses, yoghurts and pasteurized goats' milk. Available from: *SuperValu outlets throughout Cork; specialist cheese shops; On the Pig's Back, English Market, Cork City.*

Pat and Ann O'Farrell
Carrigaline Farmhouse Cheese
The Rock
Carrigaline
County Cork
Tel: 021 437 2856
Fax: 021 437 1012
Email:
carrigalinefarmhousecheese@eircom.net

Creamy cows' milk cheese in natural or herb flavours, in small or large waxed rounds. Latest addition to the range is a mildly smoked version. West Cork Fuchsia branded. Available from: *Selected SuperValu stores throughout Cork and nationwide, and small delis and independents in the county. Can also be found in certain stockists in the UK and USA. Telephone for details.*

Siobhan and Brian O'Regan
Beechwood Farm
Kinsale
County Cork
Tel: 086 8292771/ 087 276 3738

Siobhan is a terrific cook whose home-made soups, pâtés, scones and breads are simply divine. Check out the Duck Liver and Confit of Duck Pâté with Cognac, Cranberries and Pistachios, smooth, golden Butternut Squash Soup, spicy Red Pepper Soup, deeply chocolatey Brownies, or light-as-a-feather muffins just for starters! Fresh free range eggs from the farm and free range turkeys at Christmas also on offer. Available from: *Farmers' Markets in Bandon, (Saturdays), Kinsale (Tuesday mornings), Cobh (Friday mornings). Telephone orders for produce and Christmas turkeys also taken.*

Frank and Gudrun Shinnick
Fermoy Natural Cheese
Strawhall
Fermoy
County Cork
Tel: 025 31310

Raw milk farmhouse cheese made from unpasteurized milk. This has a creamy texture, punctuated with teeny holes, and a well-developed, lingering flavour. Available from: *Urru Culinary Store, Bandon, West Cork Gourmet Store, Schull; other specialist delis in the Cork area; On the Pig's Back, English Market, Cork City.*

Dick Willems

Coolea Farmhouse Cheese
Coolea
Macroom
County Cork
Tel:/Fax: 026 45204

Gouda-style cheeses made from
pasteurized cows' milk. Mild or mature
– the mature cheese has a full-bodied,
powerful flavour. Available from:
Selected SuperValu stores throughout Cork;
specialist delis and cheese shops; On the
Pig's Back, English Market, Cork City.

Home Baking

Anne Bradfield

Taste a Memory
Kinsale
County Cork
Tel: 086 8682201

Pasties, pies and tarts are Anne
Bradfield's speciality. Her Cornish
Pasties are meaty and mightily peppery,
Lamb and Feta have a taste of the
Continent, Spicy Beef have just the right
amount of chilli kick. Grab a potato-
topped meat or fish pie as well. There's
no end to this woman's pie talents!
Available from: *Kinsale Farmers' Market*
(Tuesday mornings); Bandon Farmers'
Market (Saturdays).

Susan Fehily

Fehily's Food Store
Bridge Street,
Ballineen
County Cork
Tel: 023 47173

Susan's handmade sweet tarts and
savoury quiches are to die for. Blue
Cheese and Red Onion, and Goat's
Cheese and Tomato are just two of
the range. Try her fresh lemon or egg
custard tarts, and the healthy brown
and seed breads too. Available from:
Made to order at the shop. Health breads
from the shop and Martin Carey Butchers,
South Main Street, Bandon. Christmas
cakes, puds and seasonal specialities made
to order. Café also in the shop.

Richard Graham-Leigh

RGL Patisserie
Maulanimirish
Dunmanway
County Cork
Tel: 023 55344
Email: jandrgrahamleigh@eircom.net

This English patissier creates superb
quality patisserie on a small scale. Try
the crumbly Chocolate Chip Cookies or
a swooningly heavenly Chocolate Mud
Pie, so rich it just melts in your mouth.
There's also a choice of fine biscuits,
shortbreads, cheese biscuits and other
delicate pastries to pick from, so you're
spoilt for choice. West Cork Fuchsia
branded. Available from: *Fehily's Food*
Store, Ballineen; Urru Culinary Store,
Bandon; selected independent shops and
fine food stores in the locality.

Andreas and Ingrid Haubold

Baking Emporium
Bridgemount House
Dunmanway
County Cork
Tel: 023 42560
Fax: 023 55279
Email: info@bakingemporiumltd.com
or visit www.bakingemporiumltd.com

Small farmhouse-based production
of pastries, cakes and gateaux. Special
occasion cakes made to order. Great
selection of home-baked breads,
including seed and spelt breads, rye
breads, ciabattas, etc. Outside catering
also available for private parties
and functions. West Cork Fuchsia
branded. Available from: *Selected hotels
and restaurants in Cork; SuperValu,
Dunmanway and other selected
stores; Bandon Farmers' Market
(Saturdays); Douglas Farmers' Market
(Saturdays); An Tobairín, South Main
Street, Bandon.*

Joe Hegarty

Heaven's Cakes
Brewery Building
Watergate Street
Bandon
County Cork
Tel: 021 4222775

Joe and his team create wonderful
patisserie for many specialist food
shops and their own outlets in the
English Market and Douglas. Look
out for the dinkiest, most delightful
strawberry pink meringues, French fruit
tarts and tartlets, among other things
definitely not to be missed! Available
from: *The English Market, Cork City;
Urru Culinary Store, Bandon; own shop
in Douglas; Bandon Farmers' Market
(Saturdays).*

Chrissie O'Flynn and Friends

Ballinascarthy
Bandon
County Cork
Tel: 023 39240

Chrissie and her friends formed a little
'co-op' who started baking specially
for Bandon Farmers' Market. Fondly
known amongst the market crowd as
'The Ballinascarthy Ladies', now the
girls' fame has spread. Consequently
their Saturday morning stall is always
sold out early. Queen cakes, iced buns,
chocolate profiteroles, coconut cake,
coffee gateaux, brown and fruit breads,
brack and many other lovely things are
all made with their own free range eggs.
What great Irish farmhouse baking is
all about. Limited supplies of free range
eggs, seasonal young vegetable plants
and flower arrangements also on sale.
Available from: *Bandon Farmers' Market
(Saturdays).*

Chocolates and Sweets

Gwen Lasserre

Gwen's Chocolate Shop
Main Street
Schull
West Cork
Tel: 028 27853

Gwen Lasserre has had a passion for chocolate since he first started making it as a young man of 14 in his home town in France. Now he creates handmade chocolates of the very highest quality in his shop in Schull. Fillings for his chocolate creations include Chinese ginger, French candied fruit and Italian pistachios. He also makes chocolate sculptures and seasonal specialities at Christmas and Easter. Don't miss a visit to his delightful shop. Chocolates available from: *Bantry Farmers' Market (Friday mornings); Urru Culinary Store, Bandon; West Cork Gourmet Store, Schull; and other specialist outlets.*

Mella McAuley

Mella's Fudge
Bantry
County Cork
Tel: 086 159 5949

Mella's name means honey, and very fitting since she's an expert sweet maker extraordinaire! She specializes in the finest, smoothest, all-butter fudge which has been described to me by a regular customer as just like 'the old fashioned fudge we used to eat long ago'. A real taste of yesteryear – with flavourings of chocolate, vanilla, dried fruit and nuts. Available from: *Bantry Farmers' Market (Friday mornings); Schull Farmers' Market (Sundays); Urru Culinary Store, Bandon; Fehily's Food Store, Ballineen; Manning's Emporium, Ballylicky, and other specialist outlets.*

Casey O'Connaill

O'Connaill Chocolate
The Rock
Church Road
Carrigaline
County Cork
Tel: 021 4373407
Fax: 021 4374073
Email: karuicon@hotmail.com

Cork-born chocolate maker whose selection includes truffles, bars, novelties and seasonal treats, cooking and drinking chocolate. Sweet treats for special diets too. The shop in Cork City also serves a super menu of coffees and hot chocolate drinks. Chocolate available from: *O'Connaill Chocolate, French Church Street, Cork. Also Midleton (Saturday mornings), Kinsale (Tuesday mornings). Nationwide through Superquinn and tourist centres. Mail order by telephone (retail and wholesale catering markets).*

Where to Shop

Where to Shop for Irish Artisan Produce

Many small producers, farmers and growers sell their wares direct to the public through a farmers' market. The following is a nationwide list. (It is normal for farmers' markets to set up or close down without notice. This list is up to date at time of going to press.)

Antrim

Ballymoney, Original Farmers' Market
Last Saturday in month,
11–2pm, Main Street, Castlecroft.

City Food and Garden Market
Every Saturday, 9–4pm, St George's Street.

Lisburn Market
Every Saturday.

Templepatrick Farmers' Market
Colmans Garden Centre.

Armagh

Portadown Market
Last Saturday of the month.

Carlow

Carlow
Every Saturday, 9–2pm, Potato Market.

Cavan

Belturbet Farmers' Market
McGowan's Garden (beside carpark),
Friday 4–7pm (May to October).

Cavan Farmers' Market
McCarren's Farham Road,
Cavan, Saturday 10–4pm.

Clare

Ballyvaughan
Saturday, 10–2pm.

Killaloe Farmers' Market
Between the Waters, Sunday 11–3pm.

Kilrush
Every Thursday, 9–2pm, The Square.

Ennis
Every Saturday, 8–2pm, car park,
Upper Main Street.

Shannon Farmers' Market
Town Centre, next to
Skycourt Shopping Centre,
Friday 12:30–7pm.

Cork

Ballydehob Food Market
Community Hall, Friday 10:30–12pm.

Bandon Country Market
Friday 10:30–1pm, Weir Street.

Bandon Farmers' Market
Every Saturday, 10–1pm,
The Old Market Gardens.

Bantry
Friday, 9–1pm, Main Square.

Blackwater Valley
Fortnightly on Saturdays, Nano Nagle
Centre, Ballygriffen.

Castletownbere
Monthly.

Clonakilty
Thursday, 10–2pm,
behind O'Donovans Hotel.

Coal Quay, Cork (also called
Cornmarket Street Market)
Saturday, 9–3pm Cornmarket
Street, Cork City.

Cobh
Every Friday, 10–1pm, Seafront.

Douglas
Saturday, 9:30–2pm, Douglas
Community Park.

Duhallow Farmers' Market
Kanturk, Thursday and Saturday morning,
10:30–1:30pm.

English Market, Cork City
Indoor market open Monday to
Saturday, 9–6pm, Grand Parade and
Princes Street, Cork City.

Fermoy Farmers' Market
Opposite Cork Marts,
Saturday 9–1pm.

Hosfords Market
Hosfords Garden Centre, Bandon-
Clonakilty Rd (N71). 5 miles west of
Bandon. First Sunday of every month
June to September, 12–5pm

Inchigeelagh Market
Creedons Hotel,
last Saturday of the month.

Kanturk Food Market
Behind Supervalu, Kanturk,
Thursday and Saturday, 10:30–1pm.

Kinsale
Tuesday 10–1pm, Short Quay.

Macroom
Tuesday, 9–4pm, Main Square.

Mahon Point
Thursday, 10–2pm,
Mahon Point Shopping Centre.

Midleton
Saturday, 9–1pm,
Hospital Road, Midleton.

Mitchelstown
Saturday, 9–1pm,
Main Square, Mitchelstown.

Schull
Sunday, 10–3pm, June to September,
Pier Road Car Park.

Skibbereen
Saturday, 10–2pm, Old Market Square.

Derry

Guildhall Country Fair
Last Saturday in the month.

Donegal

Ballybofey Farmers' Market
Every Friday, 12–4pm, GAA grounds.

Donegal Town Farmers' Market
Diamond, third Saturday of the month.

Down

Castlewellan Farmers' Market
Castlewellan Community Centre,
Saturday 10–1pm.

Newry Dundalk
Every Friday, 9–2pm,
Newry Marketplace, John Mitchell Place.

Dublin

Anglesea Road Village Market
Grounds of St Mary's Church,
Thursday 10–4pm.

Ballymun Farmers' Market
Ballymun Civic Centre,
first Thursday of the month,
11–2:30pm.

Dalkey
Every Friday, 10–4pm, Dalkey Town Hall.

Docklands Market
Mayor Square, IFSC,
Wednesday 11–3pm.

Dundrum
Every Saturday, 10–4pm, Airfield House.

Dun Laoghaire Harbour Market
Every Saturday, 10–4pm,
Dun Laoghaire Harbour.

Dun Laoghaire Market
Every Sunday, 11–4pm, People's Park.

Dun Laoghaire Shopping Centre
Dun Laoghaire Shopping Centre,
Thursday 10–5pm.

Farmleigh Food Market
Farmleigh House

Fingal Food Fayre
Fingal Arts Centre,
last Sunday every month, 12–5pm.

Howth Harbour
Every Saturday, 10–3pm.

Leapardstown
Every Friday, 11–7pm,
Leapardstown Racecourse.

Liffey Valley Shopping Centre
Quarryvale, D.22,
Friday 10–4pm.

Malahide
Every Saturday, 11–5pm, GAA facility,
Church Road.

Marley Park
Saturday, 10–4pm.

Monkstown Village Market
Every Saturday, 10–4pm,
Monkstown Parish Church.

Pearse Street
Saturday, 9:30–3pm, St Andrew's Centre.

Phibsborough Farmers' Market
Near Doyle's Corner,
Saturday 10–5pm (from July 21st).

Powerscourt Town Centre Market
Powerscourt Town Centre, D.2,
Friday 10–4pm.

Ranelagh
Every Sunday, 10–4pm, Multi-
denominational School.

South Dublin Co. Market
High Street, Tallaght,
Friday 10–4pm.

Swords Farmers' Market
St Colmcilles GAA Club, near Applewood
Village, Thursday 10–4pm.

The Red Stables Food Market
St Anne's Park, Clontarf
(beside the Rose Garden),
Saturday 10–5pm.

Temple Bar
Every Saturday, 9–5pm,
Meeting House Square.

Galway

Athenry Farmers' Market –
100% Organic
Market Cross, Friday 9:30–4pm.

Ballinasloe
Every Friday, 10–3pm, Croffy's Centre,
Main Street.

Galway City
Every Saturday, 8:30–4pm.

Loughrea Market
Barrack Street, Thursday 10–2pm.

Tuam Farmers Market –
100% Organic
Market Cross, Friday 9:30–4pm.

Kerry

Cahirciveen Market
Community Centre, Thursday
10–2pm, (June to September)

Caherdaniel Market
Village Hall, Friday 10–12pm
(June to September and Christmas)

Dingle
Friday, 9:30–4pm, by fishing harbour
and bus stop.

Dunloe Farmers Market
Dunloe Golf Course, Sunday 1–5pm.

Kenmare
Every Wednesday, 10–3pm, The Square.

Listowel Farmers Market
The Square, Listowel, Friday 10–2pm.

Milltown Old Church
Saturday 10–2pm,
Milltown, Organic Centre.
Tuesday–Friday 2–5pm.

Milltown Market
Organic Centre, Tuesday to Friday, 2–5pm

Listowel
Every Thursday, 10–1pm, Seanchie Centre.

Sneem
*Tuesday, 11–2pm, June to September
and Christmas, Community Centre.*

Tralee Farmers' Market
Friday 9–5pm.

Kildare

Athy Farmers Market
Emily Square, Sunday 10–2pm.

Crookstown Farmers Market
*Crookstown Inn/Shackleton,
Friday 2–7pm.*

Kildare Folly Market
*Kildare Town, third Sunday in the month,
11–6pm.*

Kildare Farmers' Market
Kildare Town, Friday 10–3pm.

Naas
*Every Saturday, 10–3pm,
The Storehouse Restaurant.*

Newbridge
*Every Friday, 10–3pm,
The Courtyard Shopping Centre.*

Maynooth Farmers Market
Maynooth, Saturday, 10–4pm.

Whitewater Farmers' Market
*Whitewater Shopping Centre, Newbridge,
Co.Kildare, Wednesday 10–4pm.*

Kilkenny

Callan Farmers' Market
*Main Street Callan, Every Saturday
10–12pm.*

Gowran Farmers' Market
*Gowran Community Hall,
third Sunday of the month 10–2pm.*

Kilkenny Farmers' Market
*Second Sunday of every month,
Gowran Park.*

Laois

Portlaoise
*Market Square Portlaoise,
Friday 10–3pm.*

Leitrim

**Original Farmers' Market
(Manorhamilton)**
*First Friday of the month, 10–2pm,
Beepark Resource Centre.*

Limerick

Abbeyfeale
Every Friday 10–1pm, Parish Hall.

Killmallock Farmers' Market
*Every Friday, 9–1pm, Kilmallock
GAA Club.*

Limerick Milk Market
*Milk Market Building, Limerick City,
Every Saturday, 7–2pm.*

Longford

Longford Farmers' Market
Every Saturday, 9:30–1pm,
Temperance Hall.

Louth

Castlebellingham
First Sunday of the month, 11–6pm,
Bellingham Castle Hotel.

Dundalk Town Producers Market
The Square, Friday 10–2pm
(From 4th August 2006).

Newry Dundalk
Every Saturday, 10–2pm, The County
Museum, Jocelyn Street, Dundalk.

Meath

Kells
Every Saturday, 10–2pm,
FBD Insurance Grounds.

Sonairte Farmers' Market, Laytown
The Ecology Centre,
3rd Sunday of the month,
10:30–5pm.

Monaghan

Monaghan Farmers' Market/
Country Market
Last Saturday of the month, 9–1pm,
Castleblayney Livestock Salesyard.

Offaly

Tullamore Country Fair
Every Saturday, 9–4pm,
Millennium Square.

The Full Moon Market
The Chestnut Courtyard,
every third Sunday.

Roscommon

Original Farmers' Market (Boyle)
Every Saturday, 10–2pm,
Grounds of King House.

Sligo

Original Farmers' Market
Every Saturday 9–1pm,
Sligo Institute of Technology Sports Field
Car Park (ample parking).

Tipperary

Cahir
Every Saturday morning,
beside The Craft Granary.

Cashel Farmers' Market
Every Friday morning, beside Cashel Mart.

Carrick-on-Suir
Heritage Centre, Main Street,
Friday 10–2pm.

Clonmel Farmers' Market
Every Saturday, 10–2pm, St Peter and St
Paul's Primary School, Kickham Street,
beside Oakville Shopping Centre.

Nenagh Farmers' Market
Every Saturday, 10–2pm, Teach an Lean.

Tyrone

Original Farmers' Market, Strabane
11–4pm, Last Saturday of the month,
The Score Centre Dock Street, Strabane.

Tyrone
8:30–1pm, First Saturday of the month,
Tesco Carpark, Dungannon.

Waterford

Ardkeen Producers Market
Ardkeen Quality Food Store,
second Sunday of every month.

Dunhill
Last Saturday of the month, 11:30–2pm,
Parish Hall.

Dungarvan
Every Thursday, 9:30–2pm, The Square.

Lismore Farmers' Market
Blackwater Valley.

Stradbally Community Market
First Saturday of the month, 10–12:30pm.

Waterford Farmers' Market
Jenkins Lane, Saturday 10–4pm.

Westmeath

Athlone Farmers' Market
Every Saturday, 10–3pm,
Market Square, Athlone.

Mullingar
Every third Sunday morning
of the month, Mullingar.

Wexford

New Ross
Every Saturday, 9–2pm, Conduit Lane.

Wexford
Every Friday, 9–2pm,
Trimmers Lane West.

Wexford Farmers' Market
Community Partnership
Every Saturday 9–2pm,
The Abbey Square Carpark.

Wexford Farmers' Market Dunbrody
Sunday 12–3:30pm,
Dunbrody Abbey Centre.

Wicklow

Bray Farmers' Market
Every Saturday, 10–3pm,
Killarney Road near the Boghall Road.

Bray Seafront Market
Friday, 10–3pm,
Albert Avenue, just across from Aquarium.

Brook Lodge Organic Market
12–5pm, Every first Sunday of the month,
Brook Lodge Inn, Macreddin.

Glendalough
Every second Sunday, 11–4pm,
Brockagh Resource Centre.

Greystones Market
Meridian Point Shopping Centre,
Saturday 10–4pm.

Kilcoole
Saturday, 10:30–11:30am.

Powerscourt Waterfall Market
Second and Fourth Sunday of the
month, Farmyard almost next to
Powerscourt Waterfall.

Wicklow Town
Market Square, Main Street,
Saturday 11–3pm.

THANA

Useful Contacts

Bord Bia
Clanwilliam Court
Mount Street lower
Dublin 2
Tel: 01 668 5155
Fax: 01 668 7521
www.bordbia.ie
Email: info@bordbia.ie

Bord Iascaigh Mhara (BIM)
Irish Sea Fisheries Board
Crofton Road
Dun Laoghaire
County Dublin
Tel: 01 214 4100
Fax: 01 284 1123
www.bim.ie
Email: info@bim.ie

Associated Craft Butchers of Ireland
Apollo Business Park
Dundrum Road
Dublin 14
Tel: 01 296 1400
Fax: 01 296 1396
www.craftbutchers.ie
Email: info@craftbutchers.ie

Slow Food Ireland
www.slowfoodireland.com

Dianne Curtin
www.diannecurtin.com
Email: dianne@diannecurtin.com

Ireland Markets
The Irish Food Market Traders
Association
Caroline Robinson (Chairperson)
Parkmore
Templemartin
Bandon
County Cork
Tel: 021 733 0178
www.irelandmarkets.com
Email: alans@nhr.net

Country Markets Ltd
Mary Beegan
Abbey House
15–17 Upper Abbey Street
Dublin 1
Tel: 01 873 5777
Email: countrymarketsltd@gmail.com

Fuchsia Foods
West Cork Leader Co-Operative
Society Ltd
South Square
Clonakilty
County Cork
Tel: 023 34035
Fax: 023 34066
www.westcorkleader.ie and
www.fuchsiabrands.com

Cork Free Choice Consumer Group
Email: carolinerobinson@eircom.net

Recipes

Thank You

To my wonderful kids Sean and Caoimhe and to my talented husband, whose stunning photography breathes life into these pages. The words would never have been enough on their own. Thank you all for your support.

To the rest of the family, for free advice and positive comments!

To my long time friend and expert cook Jill Cox and her husband David, for all our fantastic years of working and laughing together. They were really special times.

To Giana Ferguson, Ruth Healy and Anthony Creswell of Slow Food West Cork.

To Veronica Neville, Shirley Kingston and Rachel Crowley, friends and fellow farmers' market campaigners.

To Bord Bia, for the farmers' market listing.

To Mike Collins and Sophie Watson of Cork University Press, for all their help and support.

To Bite!, for design expertise.

Finally, to all the Creators who took time to share their stories with me.